Democracy

Look for these and other books in the Lucent
Overview series:

Abortion
Acid Rain
AIDS
Alcoholism
Animal Rights
The Beginning of Writing
Cancer
Collapse of the Soviet Union
Dealing with Death
Death Penalty
Democracy
Drugs and Sports
Drug Trafficking
Eating Disorders
Endangered Species
Energy Alternatives
Espionage
Extraterrestrial Life
Gangs
Garbage
The Greenhouse Effect
Gun Control
Hate Groups

Hazardous Waste
The Holocaust
Homeless Children
Illiteracy
Immigration
Ocean Pollution
Oil Spills
The Olympic Games
Organ Transplants
Ozone
Population
Prisons
Rainforests
Recycling
Reunification of Germany
Smoking
Space Exploration
Special Effects in the Movies
Teen Alcoholism
Teen Pregnancy
Teen Suicide
The UFO Challenge
The United Nations

Democracy

by Don Nardo

LUCENT
B·O·O·K·S

Library of Congress Cataloging-in-Publication Data

Nardo, Don, 1947—
  Democracy / by Don Nardo.
      p.   cm. — (Lucent overview series)
  Includes bibliographical references and index.
  Summary: Discusses the concept of democracy as it has
developed in America and abroad.
  ISBN 1-56006-147-2 (alk. paper)
  1. Democracy—Juvenile literature.   2. Democracy—United
States—Juvenile literature. [1. Democracy.]   I. Title.   II. Series.
JC433.N25   1994
321.8—dc20   93-4912
                                                                        CIP
                                                                         AC

Copyright © 1994 by Lucent Books, Inc.
P.O. Box 289011, San Diego, CA 92198-9011
Printed in the U.S.A.

Contents

Introduction

THE TWENTIETH CENTURY has seen a worldwide growth of democratic political systems. By the early 1990s a majority of the world's most powerful nations were democracies and more than seventy nations had democratic governments. Yet, the term democracy is widely misunderstood and interpreted in different ways. The meaning of democracy seems to be embodied in its root words. The term is a combination of the Greek words *demos*, meaning "people," and *kratos*, meaning "rule." From this, one might conclude that democracy means "rule of the people." But this is a vague definition. It does not say exactly which people in society should rule or how they should go about it.

Most dictionaries try to elaborate on this definition. Webster's *New Collegiate Dictionary*, for example, defines democracy as "a government in which the supreme power is vested in the people . . . directly or indirectly through a system . . . involving periodically held free elections." This is better but still incomplete. It links democracy with free elections, but other forms of government also have such elections. A republic, as defined in the same dictionary, is "a government in which supreme power resides in a body of citizens entitled to vote and is exercised by

(Opposite page) Chinese students in Taipei, Taiwan, stage a protest in 1990 to demand democratic reforms in their government. Demands for democracy resounded in many nations as the world entered the last decade of the twentieth century.

7

elected officers and representatives." Essentially, these definitions for democracy and republic are the same. Does that mean a democracy is a republic and vise versa? Which more accurately describes the United States?

Democracy or republic?

America's founders, in fact, rarely used the term democracy and referred to the early United States as a republic. One of the founders, James Madison, defined a republic as a government that protects citizens' individual rights and liberties. He and most of his colleagues described democracy as being similar but applicable only on a small scale, as in the case of the ancient Greek democracies. Each of these was scarcely larger than a city. Both systems, Madison said, share such concepts as freedom, equality, and free elections. During the nineteenth and twentieth cen-

James Madison, one of the founders of the United States, defined a republic as a government that protects individual rights and liberties.

turies, people began to ignore the differences between *democracy* and *republic*, and the terms became, more or less, interchangeable.

The terms also became subject to a wider interpretation. During the last two centuries, the age-
old system of monarchy, the absolute rule of
kings and queens, rapidly disappeared in most
parts of the world. The concept of monarchy
came to be seen as "bad," "outdated," and "unfair." On the other hand, the terms democracy and
republic came to be viewed as "good," "modern,"
and "fair." Consequently, nearly every modern
nation began calling itself either a democracy or a
republic. But this widespread usage only con-
fuses attempts to define democracy because many
who have claimed to be democratic are not. For

*America's founders gather for
the Second Continental
Congress in 1778. Most of them
thought of the United States as a
republic rather than a
democracy.*

example, few people outside of Cuba would argue that the Republic of Cuba is, in fact, a republic. And almost no one believes that the Democratic People's Republic of (North) Korea is actually democratic. These nations, like many others, are really dictatorships.

According to teacher and writer Saul K. Padover, "The current fashion in many parts of the world of referring to dictatorships as 'people's democracy'. . . is a fraud perpetrated by dictators to mislead the people." Such nations have little or no freedom, equality, or free elections. Perhaps, then, democracy can be defined as a government that does operate under these three concepts.

But such a definition would still be inadequate. Even in countries widely viewed as model democracies, such as the United States, England, and Canada, freedom and equality were, and still are, not a given. The United States, calling itself a democratic state, had slavery until the 1860s. And American women could not vote until the twentieth century. Even today, some minority groups in the United States complain that they are treated as second-class citizens. According to scholar Eli Sagan, "Democracy almost defies definition, for if we mean by 'democracy' true equality between all adult members of society, excluding neither women, nor minorities, nor the poor, then there never has been a democratic sociey."

Striving for universal freedom and equality

Nevertheless, democracies like the United States sincerely aim toward creating universal freedom and equality. They do this through elections, constitutions, and written laws. These elements do not necessarily ensure that everyone in society will be happy, well-off, or treated well. But at least they give everyone equal opportunity

A political convention attracts citizens from all walks of life. Although the United States has not achieved equality for all, its citizens are free to express their views and fully take part in the political process.

to have a say in public affairs. In 1963, President John F. Kennedy remarked, "Not every child has an equal talent . . . or equal motivation. But they should have the equal right to develop their talent and . . . to make something of themselves." Perhaps, therefore, a somewhat accurate, or at least workable, definition for democracy would be: a government which guarantees equal opportunity for everyone through free election of leaders and fair written laws.

1

The First Democracies

DEMOCRATIC GOVERNMENT originated in ancient Greece in the sixth and fifth centuries B.C. Before that time, the world's nations and empires were absolute monarchies ruled by kings. In these lands, the common people usually lived in extreme poverty and had no rights, no say in government, and no opportunity to determine their own futures. As historian Edith Hamilton put it, "The ancient world, in so far as we can reconstruct it, bears everywhere the same stamp. In Egypt . . . in Mesopotamia . . . we find the same conditions: a despot [tyrant] enthroned, whose whims and passions are the determining factor in the state; a wretched, subjugated [conquered] populace."

In such systems, the idea of equality between the ruling nobility and those they governed was unthinkable. All classes of society automatically accepted the idea that the kings and nobles were better than other people or had been chosen by the gods to rule. Consequently democratic ideas did not take root in those societies.

To the Greeks, on the other hand, the idea of absolute monarchy was alien. Between 1000 and 700 B.C., city-states rose in Greece. These tiny

(Opposite page) The ancient Greek city-state of Athens was the birthplace of democracy.

13

nations were each composed of a central town surrounded by supporting villages and farmland. At first, these city-states, like other ancient lands, were ruled by kings. But the Greeks did not view their kings with awe or reverence. Usually, a king was simply the city's wealthiest or most powerful landowner, an aristocrat, which comes from the Greek word *aristoi*, meaning "best people." In time, other landowners became equally wealthy and powerful and demanded a say in government. So, by the mid-seventh century B.C., most Greek cities had thrown out their kings and were ruled by small groups of aristocrats. This kind of government is known as an oligarchy, which means "rule of the few."

In the oligarchies of the seventh and sixth centuries B.C., the first democratic ideas, such as equality and rule by law, began to take shape. Everyone acknowledged that no ruling oligarch was better than the others. These men were, therefore, considered equal, among themselves and among the people. It was not long before

The central marketplace in an ancient Greek city-state was the site where business and social life took place. The city-states were at first ruled only by the wealthy landowners, but gradually the rights of other citizens were also recognized.

other prominent citizens in some city-states began to assert that they were just as good as the oligarchs. These citizens demanded that they too have a say in government.

The idea of many individuals in the community having a political voice grew increasingly popular. A few city-states developed assemblies, groups of well-to-do citizens that met periodically to discuss social and political affairs. Although some assemblies offered advice to the ruling oligarchs, these men did not have to act on the advice. So these early assemblies had no real political power. Nevertheless, ordinary citizens' demands for a say in government continued to grow, and eventually these demands resulted in systems of law. According to historian Victor Ehrenberg, in many Greek city-states:

> political individualism developed out of the tensions of social life. . . . There was, on the one hand, the urgent demand of the ordinary peasants no longer to be the victims of the . . . [rule] of the aristocrats. . . . Oppression and injustice were causes of growing complaint, and the first remedy was the codification [compiling] of law. . . . In various parts of the Greek world laws were written down for the first time. . . . Laws relating to the family, the rights of inheritance, and the position of slaves and foreigners were among the matters which increasingly became the concern of the state. . . . Hence eventually sprang the idea . . . that the community . . . was based on the rule of law.

Athens takes the lead

Athens became the first Greek city-state to reform its government by instituting a widespread system of laws. This was the first major step in the development of Athenian democracy, which occurred by degrees over a period of nearly two centuries. Athens was already the most populous, progressive, and influential city-state in Greece.

Therefore, it held onto its lead in introducing political reform and became a model for other Greek democracies.

Athens's first set of laws was drawn up in 621 B.C. by an oligarch named Draco. Although everyone considered the introduction of these laws to be a major reform, the laws themselves were almost immediately unpopular. This was because many of the laws were unusually harsh. One of the worst of the laws allowed creditors to enslave their debtors if the debtors were unable to repay what they owed. Demands for reforming Draco's laws became widespread by the beginning of the sixth century B.C.

This reform came at the hands of a popular ruler named Solon, whom later Greeks remembered as the first great champion of democratic ideals. The Greek philosopher and writer Aristotle wrote, "Now, as to Solon, there are those that see him as a truly radical reformer who put an end to an over-extreme oligarchy, released the body of the people from subjugation, and estab-

Athenian citizens gather in a body known as the Assembly to debate and decide issues of law and government.

lished the excellent constitutional blend which they call 'the ancestral democracy.'"

In 594 B.C. Solon became archon, or chief administrator, of Athens. He immediately changed many of the unpopular laws, especially the one which enslaved debtors. Solon not only made it illegal for creditors to enslave debtors, but also freed all debtors who had been enslaved. He also put important restraints on government by making those in power accountable under the law for corrupt practices while in office.

Solon's most important governmental reform was the division of the citizenry into four classes, according to wealth and property ownership. As had always been the case in Athens, only those born into the four prominent tribes thought to have originally founded the city were considered citizens. People from other tribes, as well as foreigners and slaves, were ineligible for citizenship. And although women in the four tribes were con-

Ancient Greek women work at household tasks. Though citizens, women could not take part in government.

The Greek political reformer Solon points to the laws he has created and urges the Athenians to follow them. He is remembered as an early champion of Greek democratic ideals.

sidered citizens, they could not hold office. Under Solon's new class system, only male citizens in the wealthiest class could hold office. But men in the lower classes gained the right to attend the Athenian Assembly, which was steadily gaining in importance, prestige, and political influence. This paved the way for more democratic government by allowing a larger portion of the citizenry to take part in political affairs.

The ancient Greek writer Plutarch explained the importance of Solon's breakdown of the citizenry:

> Solon took a survey of the estates of the citizens, intending to leave the great offices [of government] in the hands of the rich but to give the rest of the people a share in other departments which they had not had before. Such as had a yearly income of five hundred measures in wet and dry

goods he placed in the first rank. . . . The second [rank] consisted of those that could keep a horse or whose lands produced three hundred measures. . . . And those of the third class . . . had but two hundred measures. . . . The rest [members of the fourth class] were . . . not admitted to any office; they had only the right to appear and cast their vote in the general Assembly of the people. This seemed at first but a slight privilege, but afterwards showed itself a matter of great importance, for most cases came at last [several decades later] to be decided by them.

Common citizens also acquired the right to sit on juries along with the upper classes to decide on the guilt or innocence of those accused of breaking the city's laws.

Under Solon's reforms, Athens was still an oligarchy. But it was one in which the leaders were bound by written laws and influenced by the will of a large proportion of citizens. By creating a system in which everyone, regardless of wealth and power, was subject to the restrictions of law, Solon had opened the way for true democracy. Solon himself summed up the importance of all people in society obeying the laws:

These are the lessons which my heart bids me teach the Athenians, how that lawlessness brings innumerable ills to the state, but obedience to the law shows forth all things in order and harmony and at the same time sets shackles on the unjust. It smooths what is rough, checks greed, dims arrogance, withers the opening blooms of ruinous folly, makes straight the crooked judgment, tames the deeds of insolence, puts a stop to the works of civil dissension [unrest], and ends the wrath of bitter strife. Under its [the law's] rule all things among mankind are sane and wise.

The voice of the people

The next major step in the evolution of Athenian democracy occurred in 508 B.C. when a citizen named Cleisthenes became the city's most

An Athenian statesman addresses members of the ruling council. The members were chosen by lot from all the male citizens of Athens.

powerful and popular political leader. Cleisthenes introduced a new constitution, or governmental and legal structure, for the state. This constitution was unwritten but the Athenians followed its basic principles for the next three centuries.

Under the constitution, Cleisthenes extended the right of citizenship to all free males eighteen years or older born in the city, regardless of tribe. All of the citizens could meet and vote in the Assembly to make or change any laws. Although still considered citizens, women could not attend the Assembly and vote.

Each year the members of the Assembly elected ten generals, called *strategoi*, to defend the city and command the military. Three archons and other officials to run the city-state were chosen yearly by lot, or random drawing, from a pool of citizen names. Cleisthenes also established the Council, a group of five hundred citizens who were also chosen yearly by lot. The Council's members suggested and prepared laws and then presented them to the Assembly, where they would be debated and voted upon.

Thus, by instituting a system in which the people made the laws and chose their own leaders, Athens became the world's first democracy. The system, as practiced in ancient Athens, is now referred to as "direct democracy" because all male citizens, through the right to meet in the Assembly, participated directly in government affairs. According to scholar Anthony Arblaster, the Assembly was the core of Athens's democracy because it:

> took the final decisions about policy. It was the sovereign [supreme and independent] body, and it was composed of all the citizens. It met, under normal circumstances, ten times a year. It was the concrete embodiment [working example] of the principle of popular sovereignty: not the people *choosing* a government once every four or five or seven years, but the people continuously governing themselves from month to month and year to year. Estimates of the size of the Athenian citizen body vary, but there were probably never more than 50,000 citizens. No doubt any one meeting was attended by half or less than half of the citizens.

Everyone equal before the law

In the following years, the Athenians continued to experiment with and perfect their democratic government. In the 480s B.C., they instituted the system of ostracism. This system allowed the public, through a popular vote, to temporarily banish a fellow citizen who had caused offense. Ostracism kept unpopular rulers from remaining in power and stopped powerful men from hurting the city by imposing their will on elected leaders.

The Athenians used bits of broken pottery like these as voting ballots in the process of ostracism.

The Athenian statesman Pericles introduced the idea of paying those who held government jobs so that the poor as well as the rich could do public service.

The process began with citizens meeting in the marketplace to write the names of those they wanted removed from power. They wrote the names on pieces of broken pottery called *ostrakons*. (The word *ostracism* comes from this term.) If six thousand or more people wrote a person's name, he was banished from the city for a period of ten years.

One of the most important democratic reforms concerned payment for government service. In the first few decades after Cleisthenes' introduction of direct democracy, many Athenians complained that the system discriminated against the poor. It was not that the laws disallowed poor people from serving in public office. Any citizen was eligible to become an archon or other official. The problem was that government jobs did not pay. Since poor people could not afford to quit their jobs to serve, nearly all public offices were held by well-to-do individuals, clearly an unfair situation.

The problem was remedied in 458 B.C., three years after a young man named Pericles rose to prominence as a political leader in Athens. Pericles was a wise and fair man who believed that Athens's greatest strength did not rest in its armies and navies. Instead, he felt the city's strength lay in the devotion and patriotism of its people. The more voice the people had in the government that controlled their lives and destinies, he reasoned, the more willing they would be to fight and die for that government. Poor people, constituting the largest single group in society, were expected to fight for their country just as well-to-do people were. Yet the poor were effectively excluded from serving in government.

Pericles delivers his famous funeral oration in which he praises the unique democratic system of government in Athens.

In Pericles' view, this inequity only weakened the state. So he introduced payment for government service, allowing any citizen, even the poorest, to hold public office. Athens was now a democracy in every sense of the word.

Pericles summed up the pride he and most other Athenians felt for their democratic government in his famous funeral oration, delivered in 431 B.C. in honor of a group of Athenian war dead. "Let me say," he declared:

> that our system of government does not copy the institutions of our neighbors. It is more the case of our being a model to others, than of our imitating anyone else. Our constitution is called a democracy because power is in the hands not of a minority but of the whole people. When it is a question of settling private disputes, everyone is equal before the law: when it is a question of putting one person before another in positions of public responsibilty, what counts is not membership of a particular class, but the actual ability which the man possesses. No one, so long as he has it in him to be of service to the state, is kept in political obscurity because of poverty. And, just as our political life is free and open, so is our day-to-day life in our relations with each other. . . . We are free and tolerant in our private lives; but in public affairs we keep to the law. This is because it commands our deep respect. . . . Here each individual is interested not only in his own affairs but in the affairs of the state as well: even those who are mostly occupied with their own business are extremely well-informed on general politics—this is a peculiarity of ours: we do not say that a man who takes no interest in politics is a man who minds his own business; we say that he has no business here at all.

The fruits of freedom

Athens had taken a bold step. It had successfully implemented a democratic system of government, which no other nation had ever before considered, much less attempted. Other Greek city-states copied the Athenian model and instituted their own democracies. Syracuse, Argos, Elis, Mantinea, and many others had democratic governments at one time or another. But none were as successful or long-lived as that of Athens. This was partly because Athens's power, prestige, and wealth allowed it, at least most of the time, to maintain its chosen system even in the face of foreign aggression. Many smaller, weaker democracies eventually fell to states ruled by kings or oligarchs.

Athens's democracy was also successful because it allowed an unprecedented degree of personal freedom. As Pericles had foreseen, this

An actor in ancient Athens tries on masks for a role. Theater and other arts blossomed in Athens during the time of Pericles because of the freedom and tolerance allowed by Athenian democracy.

freedom made Athenians of all walks of life fiercely loyal and willing to defend the state. Complete freedom also made the city extremely attractive to people from other city-states and nations. Architects, scientists, teachers, painters, sculptors, and playwrights from many lands flocked to Athens. During the brief years of Pericles' rule, the city enjoyed a cultural golden age, creating buildings, statues, and literature that have awed and inspired the world ever since. Commenting on how Athens thrived on democratic freedom, historian W.G. Hardy wrote:

> There was no censorship in fifth-century B.C. Athens. Rather there was an almost unparalleled freedom of speech as well as of thought. In the midst of the bitter [Peloponnesian] war against Sparta [a city-state run by kings], Aristophanes [the playwright] was permitted to satirize [poke fun at] the generals of Athens, and the great Pericles himself, on the stage, and to plead for peace. He was not put in jail. Instead he won first prizes [in theatrical contests]. . . . The freedom which the Athenians enjoyed was a rare thing in antiquity [ancient times]—or, for that matter, in modern times. That feeling of freedom was, perhaps, the chief reason why Athenians, to paraphrase Pericles, fell in love with their city, and why Athens became an education to [Greece] and the world and not a little of the tremendous outburst of art and literature in fifth-century B.C. Athens must be attributed to the liberty in speech, thought, and action which its citizens enjoyed. The bell-like keynote of the world's first democracy was freedom.

Why Greek democracy failed

But despite all of its benefits and fairness, Athenian democracy did not last. Sparta defeated Athens in 404 B.C. at the end of the Peloponnesian War, a conflict that engulfed nearly all of the Greek city-states. The Spartans dismantled Athens's democracy and replaced it with an oligarchy. Only a few years later, however, Sparta's

power declined and the Athenians reinstated their democracy. The system then remained in effect until the second century B.C. when Rome conquered Greece. The Romans made Greece a province of their empire and the daring Greek experiments with democratic government ended for good. At the time, no one could have guessed that democracy would not return to the world for some nineteen centuries.

Why did Greek democracy fail? The simplest answer is that Athens and the other democratic states were conquered by nondemocratic nations. But this does not explain why no other nations copied the Greek idea and instituted democracies in the following decades and centuries. The real question is: Why did democracy, once introduced, fail to take root and spread in the ancient world?

"One answer to the question," says Saul Padover, "is that, at the stage of history when democracy first appeared, [humanity] was not ready for it, hence its continuity was not possible." Padover explains that early democratic experiments broke down because democracy is based largely on the concept of individual liberty, and most ancient people were group-oriented. In other words, ancient people did not appreciate the idea of the individual person having worth. For example, the Romans and other ancients saw the individual as a part of something larger and far more important—society itself. While the Athenians conceived of society as working solely for the good of each individual, others saw each individual as working only for the good of society. Therefore, democracy worked in Athens and some other Greek states because the concept of individualism developed in these places. But it was an idea far ahead of its time.

A "radical" concept

Indeed, even many Greeks were not ready to embrace the ideas of equality and freedom inherent in the concept of democracy. The great thinkers Plato and Aristotle saw many good things in democracy. But they also still believed that some people are naturally more virtuous and intelligent, and therefore better, than others, and that these people should rule. In a democracy, Aristotle argued, power rests with the "mob," the masses of uneducated poor. "A democracy is a government in the hands of men of low birth, poverty, and vulgar employments," he wrote in his book *Politics*. And as Plato put it in the *Republic:*

> Freedom creates rather more drones [lazy, dim-witted people] in the democratic . . . state. In a

democracy they are almost the entire ruling power, and while the keener [more intelligent] sort speak and act, the rest keep buzzing about the beam and do not suffer a word to be said on the other side; hence in democracies almost everything is managed by the drones.

Today, such ideas are usually seen as arrogant, unfair, and blatantly prejudiced. But in ancient times, the vast majority of those with money and power thought this way. And nearly everyone, regardless of wealth, took for granted such concepts as slavery and men being superior to women. The world simply was not ready to embrace the "radical" concept of equality and freedom for all. It is not surprising, therefore, that the Greek democracies did not last or take root.

However, Athens's brief but magnificent experiment in human freedom was not in vain. Nearly two thousand years after Greek democracy disappeared, the world rediscovered it. And it was a different world, one in which the concepts of individual worth and human freedom were gaining widespread popularity. The Greek democratic achievement became a brilliant and inspiring model to be studied and imitated. Amazingly, Pericles himself had correctly predicted this turn of events. "Future ages will wonder at us," he declared, "as the present age wonders at us now."

Aristotle, whose philosophy has deeply influenced Western civilization, believed that democracy was government largely by the ignorant and poor and thus far from ideal.

2

The Development
of Modern
Democratic Ideas

AFTER ROME ABSORBED Greece in the second century B.C., democracy disappeared from the world for almost two thousand years. Not until the American and French revolutions of the late 1700s did democratic government finally reappear. Yet the long interval without democracy was important to the development of modern democracy. During those centuries, several significant social and legal concepts, institutions, and practices slowly evolved across Europe. These eventually led to and inspired the American, French, and other modern experiments with democracy. The most important of these concepts included the idea of restraints on government through a constitution, a belief in the existence of natural laws affecting everyone in society, and the notion of representative government.

(Opposite page) A legislator in ancient Rome addresses the senate. Although Rome was not a democracy, the Roman concept of law formed much of the basis of modern ideas of law and justice.

Democracy rejected

The long absence of democracy was caused by a number of factors. Most societies were still group-oriented and did not recognize the impor-

31

The Greek philosopher Plato believed that government by the aristocracy was superior to a democracy.

tance, worth, and rights of the individual. Also, the concept that certain people were "born" or "divinely inspired" to rule others remained strong. This made the ideas of social equality and of common people taking part in government hard to accept. And it did not help that most of the pro-democratic writings of ancient Greece were lost over the centuries. On the other hand, the works of Aristotle and Plato, which were largely antidemocratic, did survive. These writings eventually became much studied and revered among Europe's upper classes and did much to discourage the notion of democracy. "If democracy was discussed at all," Saul Padover explains:

> it was either as an irrelevancy [unimportant matter] or as a bad example. At best, it was misunderstood; at worst it was spurned and maligned [rejected]. The presumed irrelevance of democracy derived from the widespread opinion that, at most, it was applicable only to small communities [like the Greek city-states]. . . . From this assumption it followed that democracy . . . could not possibly be considered as a practical [system] for a sizable nation.

But despite widespread scorn for and misunderstanding of democracy, the seeds of modern democratic thought were slowly growing. Some of these ideas concerned constitutions and laws. In most ancient societies, a constitution was largely an established set of laws and political procedures made by a monarch or group of oligarchs. The purpose was to ensure control and efficient rule of the common people. A constitution, therefore, was designed to restrain the governed rather than the government. Nevertheless, in some early societies, once laws were written down, the idea arose that certain laws derived from nature or from a god or gods. Some of the most basic examples were commandments that people do right rather than wrong and that they refrain from murdering and stealing. Such laws, it appeared, were meant to apply to everyone, rulers and subjects alike. This is known as the doctrine of natural law.

The legacy of Roman law

One of the most important original sources of the idea of natural law was ancient Rome. At first, Rome, which controlled the European world for many centuries after conquering Greece, called itself a republic. It had two assemblies that made laws. It also had two consuls, or heads of state, that administered these laws and a senate,

Roman senators ceremonially enter the halls of the senate. The idea that all persons were subject to natural law was inherent in Roman law.

Famed Roman orator Cicero speaks to the citizens of Rome. Cicero firmly believed in the existence and authority of natural law.

or group of legislators, that advised the consuls. But Rome never became a democratic state. This was because the wealthy and powerful senators used their influence to control the consuls and assemblies. Since most power rested in the hands of a privileged few, Rome was really an oligarchy.

But the Roman Republic did develop an impressive set of laws that was supposed to apply fairly to everyone. Even though such fairness did not always occur in practice, the very idea that it *should* occur formed the basis for natural law. The chief commentator of this concept was the Roman writer and legislator Cicero. He believed that the gods had ordained certain concepts of right and wrong that applied to people everywhere. No person, not even a ruler, he reasoned, could make wrong right or right wrong. In his work the *Republic*, Cicero wrote:

> There is in fact a true law—namely, right reason—which is in accordance with nature, applies to all men, and is unchangeable and eternal. By its commands this law summons men to the performance of their duties; by its prohibitions it restrains them from doing wrong. . . . Neither the senate nor the people can absolve [relieve] us from our obligation to obey this law . . . and there will be, as it were, one common master and ruler of men, namely God, who is the author of this law, its interpreter, and its sponsor. The man who will not obey it will abandon his better self, and, in denying the true nature of man, will thereby suffer the severest of penalties, though he has escaped all the other consequences which men call punishments.

Although logical and noble, Cicero's ideas about natural law were discussed almost exclusively in small academic, or literary, circles and had no effect on Roman politics.

The Roman Republic fell and the Roman Empire, under the absolute rule of emperors, took its place in the first century B.C. Although Rome was now essentially a monarchy, it retained a constitution in the form of the large body of law inherited from its republican days. The concept that the constitution contained natural, god-given laws was also assumed in the process. However, this concept was still academic and did not alter the great power the emperors wielded. Still, the idea remained.

When Rome adopted Christianity as the official state religion in the fourth century A.D., the concept of natural law gained increased attention. Christian beliefs were rooted in the Jewish writings of the Old Testament, which placed God's laws above those of humans. And the Christians,

A group of early Christians gathers in ancient Rome. When Rome adopted Christianity as its state religion, the Christian ideal of individual worth melded with the Roman idea of natural law.

like the ancient Greeks, emphasized the dignity and worth of the individual, regardless of wealth. As scholar Carl J. Friedrich wrote:

> probably the most distinctive religious root of modern constitutionalism is the Christian belief in the dignity and worth of each person, each human being, no matter how lowly. For if we ask what is the political function of a constitution, we find that the core objective is that of safeguarding each member of the political community as such a person. . . . The constitution is meant to protect the *self*. . . . This preoccupation with the self, rooted in Christian beliefs, eventually gave rise to the notion of rights which were thought to be natural.

Perhaps in time the Romans might have translated this idea of basic human rights into political change and developed democratic government. However, they never got the chance. In the late fifth century, Rome fell to waves of European barbarian tribes.

The feudal kingdoms

The thousand years following Rome's fall is referred to as medieval times, or the Middle Ages. During this period, many small kingdoms dotted Europe. Most of these states were ruled by various kings, nobles, and warlords under the feudal system. In the feudal system, a wealthy and powerful lord allowed the poor peasants to work his land in exchange for a share of the bounty and service in the lord's army. Because the people had no say in government, feudal societies were decidedly undemocratic.

But the European kingdoms inherited and used many Roman ideas and institutions, especially Roman law and the Christian church. Thus, from the beginning, feudal societies were ingrained with the notion of natural law. This placed at least some restraint on the medieval kings and lords. People recognized and feared their consid-

erable powers. But they also saw the kings and lords as human beings who were, like everyone else, subject to certain divinely inspired laws. One of the first known writers to point out that kings were bound by certain laws was the twelfth-century English judge Henry de Bracton. In his work entitled, *On the Laws and Customs of the English*, he declared that:

> the king has a superior, namely God. Likewise, the law, by which he was made king. And likewise his court, to wit, the counts and barons [nobles], for the counts are called, as it were, the king's associates, and he who has an associate has a master. Thus if the king should be without a bridle [restraint for horses], that is, without the law, they ought to put a bridle on him.

Bracton's view that rulers should be subject to natural law was similar to Cicero's except on one important point. Cicero implied that rulers who

An illustration from a thirteenth-century French prayerbook depicts peasants tending cattle and picking fruit. Though they had no political power, the people believed that kings were subject to divine law.

went beyond the law would be punished or restrained by God. By contrast, Bracton suggested that *people* have the right to apply such restraints. This introduced the democratic idea of the governed having some kind of legal means against unjust rulers.

The democratic idea of government decisions being made by representatives of the people also had its roots in medieval feudal times. The Roman Empire had been a strong, highly organized state with the center of government in one or two places. That made dictatorial rule by an emperor fairly easy. The emperor simply made his wishes known and, if necessary, sent his army out to enforce them. By contrast, the typical medieval European kingdom was a disorganized patchwork of large estates and cities, each overseen by a powerful local lord. The king of such a realm rarely had a stronger military than the lords and nobles he ruled. Therefore, his power depended on the goodwill and allegiance of his leading subjects. With the nobles' loyalty he was strong. Without it, he was weak and unable to rule effectively.

In order to secure the allegiance of the nobles, the feudal kings evolved the custom of periodically calling them together. These "Great Councils," or "estates," were meetings in which the most powerful in society discussed the issues of the day. They then made their wishes on these matters known to the king. A king was not bound by these wishes. But a prudent ruler who wanted to keep his subjects' allegiance and retain power usually went along with the popular consensus.

In a sense, each attending member of a Great Council represented his own district or city. When a royal policy benefited a local lord, the peasants under that lord usually benefited, too. So, even though the common people had no direct say in government, they did have a representative looking after their interests. Thus, the kingdom-wide councils were the forerunners of the parliaments, or representative lawmaking assemblies, that govern most modern democracies.

England leads the way

The feudal concepts of natural law and local representation eventually began to have a profound impact on the structure of government. The first important political reform occurred in England in the thirteenth century. Other reforms quickly followed, and for several centuries afterward, England led the way in developing democratic ideals and institutions.

The first important reform was the signing of a document called the Magna Carta, or "great charter," by King John in the year 1215. When King

John decided to impose some unusually heavy taxes, the lords of the realm rejected the idea. They were used to paying only certain customary taxes. They claimed that John was exceeding his authority under the fair and natural "law of the land" which bound him as well as them. Political scholar Strathearn Gordon explains that:

> on a stormy day . . . on the marshy islet of Runnymede, a committee of twenty-five angry nobles extorted [forced] from their reluctant King a promise that in the future he would adhere to the law of the land by refraining from imposing any feudal aid (tax), except the . . . customary ones . . . *save* [except] *by the common council of the realm.* Thus was the doctrine of the necessity of consent firmly re-established.

For the first time, the powers of the king had been curbed officially, in writing. And the change was permanent. From that time on, English kings needed the consent of a council of their subjects before enacting changes that affected the entire realm.

At first, the royal councils were composed strictly of nobles and other wealthy landowners. But this soon changed. In 1295, King Edward I called a council which later became known as the "Model Parliament." The council members included forty-nine powerful lords and several archbishops and bishops, who represented the interests of the church. In addition, these members brought with them two representatives from each city and shire, or county. These lesser members, or "commons," were elected locally by their fellow citizens. "Thus," said Strathearn Gordon:

> the assembly [parliament] had ceased to be a feudal court, dependent entirely upon land tenure [ownership], and was becoming a body in which every class and interest had a voice. It was an assembly of . . . 'those who pray, those who fight and those who work.'

King John signs England's Magna Carta in 1215. This "great charter" was England's first written law limiting a king's powers.

In the next two or three centuries, the English Parliament gained increasing importance. Eventually, its powers would overshadow those of the English monarchs.

During these same years, as the Middle Ages ended, other European kingdoms rose, fell, and combined. By the 1400s, 1500s, and 1600s, the kingdoms evolved into large and powerful monarchies such as Spain, France, and Russia, all rivals of England. Many of these nations colonized other parts of the world, including Africa, Australia, and North and South America. The colonists usually were subjects of the mother country's king and had little or no say in government. Lands outside of Europe's influence, such as Japan and

A thirteenth-century drawing of a meeting of the English parliament. Within a few centuries of its creation, the English parliament would assume greater authority than that of the king or queen.

China, continued to be ruled by emperors. So, still no democracies existed in the world.

The powerful European nations were undergoing dramatic social and economic changes between the 1400s and 1700s. Increased trade and colonization opened up new economic markets around the world. A larger, richer, and more powerful middle class of merchants emerged. The members of this "mercantile" class felt that they, like the nobles, should have a say in government. Another important development was the invention of the printing press in the fifteenth century. Before, only wealthy people could afford to be educated and own books. But with the use of the printing press, books could be made and sold cheaply. Thus, books were easily available, and many common people learned to read and thereby gained access to the ideas of writers and philosophers.

Among these writers were political thinkers who increasingly advocated governmental reform. The writers especially called for changes that gave the common people a greater share in the decision making. England's still-developing parliamentary system had already partially achieved this goal. So, many of the most progressive political writers were English.

One of the most influential English political writers was John Locke. He advocated that human beings have certain God-given rights, among them life, liberty, and property. When rulers threaten or violate these rights, said Locke, the people have a right to replace those rulers. Thus, the political authority of the state derives from and rests with the people. Further, the way to prevent rulers from becoming abusive is to separate governmental powers. If the executive, or administrative, powers and the legislative, or lawmaking, powers remain in separate hands, Locke said, no one person or group can wield abusive power. In his *Second Treatise of Civil Government*, written in 1690, Locke declared that:

> The great and chief end [goal] . . . of men's uniting into common wealths [nations], and putting themselves under government, is the preservation of their property [including their life and liberty]. . . . Absolute . . . power, or governing without settled standing laws, can neither of them [fulfill] the ends of society and government, which men would not quit the freedom of the state of nature for, and tie themselves up under, were it not to preserve their lives, liberties, and fortunes. . . . The supreme power [of the state] cannot take from any man any part of his property without his own consent. For the preservation of property . . . [is] the end of government, and that for which men enter into society.

Another popular political writer, Frenchman Charles de Montesquieu, agreed with and spread Locke's ideas about government. Montesquieu

Seventeenth-century English philosopher John Locke wrote that the political authority of the state derives from and rests with the common people.

extended the concept of separating governmental power to include the judiciary, or the courts and judges. In his 1748 work *The Spirit of the Laws,* he stated:

> There is no liberty . . . where judicial power is not separated from both legislative and executive power. If judicial and legislative power are not separated, power over the life and liberty of citizens would be arbitrary [subject to the whims of the powerful], because the judge would also be the legislator. . . . All would be lost if the same men . . . exercised these three powers—that of making laws, that of executing public decisions, and that of judging the crimes and disputes of private persons.

The will of the people

Perhaps the most influential and controversial political theorist of the period was the Swiss-French writer Jean-Jacques Rousseau. Inspired by the ancient Greeks, he championed the idea of direct democracy. Like Locke and Montesquieu, he believed that the people are the source of political authority. According to Rousseau, the people's wishes, or the "general will," is what should drive the engines of government. No law is legitimate, he argued, unless it expresses the general will. The people, he said, should meet, make laws, and vote in local assemblies, such as town meetings. The government must be totally subordinate to and run by the people. In his monumental 1762 work *The Social Contract*, Rousseau made the now famous statement, "Man is born free; and everywhere he is in chains." Explaining his idea of popular government, he continued:

> Each of us puts his person and all his power in common under the supreme direction of the general will, and, in our corporate [collective] capacity, we receive each member as an indivisible part of the whole. At once, in place of the individual personality of each contracting [participating]

French philosopher Charles de Montesquieu endorsed Locke's idea of separating the government's powers to make and execute laws.

party, this act of association creates a moral and collective body, composed of as many members as the assembly contains voters, and receiving from this act its unity, its common identity, its life and its will.

The writings of Locke, Montesquieu, Rousseau, and others had an enormous impact in many educated circles in Europe and in European colonies around the world. In many of these places, the desire for political reform grew increasingly fervent. By the mid-1700s, democratic ideas, such as the doctrine of natural law and political representation, resulted in sweeping changes in Britain. Parliament controlled all law-making and finances, and the king had extremely limited powers. But some people wanted to go further and implement the more radical ideas of Locke and other writers.

The growing desire for liberty, equality, and government run by the people would eventually translate into action in 1776 in Britain's American colonies. After a long absence from the world's political arena, democracy was about to make an explosive comeback.

Jean-Jacques Rousseau advocated direct democracy, or rule by the people themselves, not by their representatives.

3

The Bold American Experiment

(Opposite page) The committee chosen to draft America's Declaration of Independence included (from left to right) Benjamin Franklin, Thomas Jefferson, John Adams, Robert Livingston, and Roger Sherman. The document is still invoked as the model of democratic ideals.

ESTABLISHING THE UNITED STATES in the late 1700s marked an important historical milestone. The U.S. political system was the world's first modern democratic government. The United States was also the world's first large democracy. Of the ancient Greek democracies, Athens was by far the largest, with a population of about 250,000 people. By contrast, in the 1780s, when the U.S. government was created, about 3 million people were living in the infant United States.

For centuries, most educated people had accepted the views of Aristotle, Plato, and other conservative writers. Democracy, they said, was a quaint, outdated idea that could not work on a scale as large as that of the United States. Even Rousseau, the chief eighteenth-century advocate of democracy, was critical. He insisted that democratic government would be effective only when instituted and controlled by small local assemblies, such as town meetings.

But the bold American democratic experiment proved the critics wrong. The U.S. government showed itself to be both workable and effective. It was not completely democratic at the outset. But the U.S. Constitution and laws ensured certain basic liberties and human rights and allowed the people a measurable voice in governing themselves. Over time, the highly flexible system grew stronger, more effective, and increasingly democratic in character. With the success of the U.S. experiment, other peoples were inspired to fight for democratic ideals. American democracy, therefore, began a worldwide trend toward democratic ideals and governments that continues today.

Colonial anger

Despite the ultimate success of America's democratic government, colonial leaders did not originally intend to establish a democracy, or even a new country. Since their founding in the 1600s, the British colonies in America had been subject to the British king and Parliament. Each colony had its own local legislature. The first and most famous was Virginia's House of Burgesses,

The first and most famous American colonial legislature, Virginia's House of Burgesses, met in this building in Williamsburg.

created in 1619. The colonial legislatures were modeled after Parliament and retained basic, long-held British democratic concepts, such as the doctrine of natural law. The legislatures were composed of representatives of the people. But, as was the case with Parliament, few people besides wealthy landowners had the right to vote. So, the legislatures were not democracies. The colonists appeared content to maintain these local governing bodies under British rule and to remain as British subjects as long as the mother country treated them fairly.

Outrageous laws and policies

However, most colonists eventually came to feel that the king and Parliament were *not* treating them fairly. After winning the French and Indian War against France in 1763, Britain gained huge territories in North America. These included southern Canada and the land stretching from the original thirteen colonies in the east, westward to the Mississippi River. To establish more control over their American possessions, British authorities began passing new and more restrictive colonial laws and policies.

In 1763, the British stationed a standing army in North America and soon afterward demanded that colonists allow British troops to stay in their homes. The British also forbade colonists from settling west of the Appalachian Mountains. And in 1765, Parliament passed the Stamp Act, placing heavy taxes on colonial newspapers, legal papers, and other documents.

Not surprisingly, the colonists strongly objected to these measures. Because they had no direct representatives in Parliament, they felt the British government had no right to tax them and regulate local colonial matters. This was the origin of the phrase "No taxation without represen-

The British government ruled in 1765 that stamps like these must be bought and placed on all legal and public documents in the American colonies. The colonists deemed this an unfair tax and protested.

tation." Colonial anger and unrest led the British to repeal the Stamp Act in 1766.

But Parliament soon enacted other outrageous laws and policies. Among them were the 1767 Townshend Acts, which taxed paint, paper, and tea, and an increase in British troop levels in Boston, New York, and other colonial cities. Colonial unrest continued to grow, and many Americans threatened violence. The British reacted in 1774 by passing the Intolerable Acts, which closed Boston Harbor to all commerce and limited the powers of local legislatures.

Kings, the servants of the people?

Bitter over what they believed were British abuses, colonial leaders met in Philadelphia in September 1774 in what became known as the First Continental Congress. Their goal was to decide the most effective way to deal with these abuses. Even at this stage, few colonists advocated a split with Britain. Most wanted only for Parliament and the king to act more reasonably. Colonial leaders like Thomas Jefferson and John Adams desired a fair settlement with the British and reaffirmed their loyalty to the mother country.

In his *Summary View of the Rights of British America*, Jefferson called for granting the colonies a larger measure of self-rule. Though his writing was directed at the king, George III, the plea was really aimed at powerful members of Parliament, since the king was already largely a figurehead:

> Kings are the servants, not the proprietors [owners] of the people. Open your breast, sire, to liberal and expanded thought. Let not the name of George the third be a blot on the page of history. . . . The great principles of right and wrong are legible [clear] to every reader; to pursue them requires not the aid of many counsellors. The whole art of government consists in the art of being honest. Only

George III was king of England in 1776 when the United States declared its independence.

Bostonians in 1774 show their displeasure with Britain's unfair taxation by publicly humiliating the tax collector.

aim to do your duty, and mankind will give you credit where you fail. . . . We are willing, on our part, to sacrifice every thing which reason can ask to the restoration of that tranquility for which all must wish. . . . This, sire, is our last, our determined resolution.

British leaders rejected this plea for reasonable compromise, however, and insisted the colonies obey all British laws and policies. Open hostilities between the colonists and British began in April 1775. Members of the Massachusetts militia clashed with British soldiers in Lexington and Concord, initiating the American revolutionary war.

A statement of principles

Colonial leaders now faced some crucial decisions. It was clear that if they were successful in their war with Britain they would then establish a new and independent country. But what kind of government should the new nation have? At first, no one was sure. The American founders had read the works of Locke, Montesquieu, Rousseau, and others calling for the recognition of basic human rights and liberties. But of these, only Rousseau advocated the radical idea of democracy. The others, especially Locke, talked about

A confrontation in 1775 between British soldiers and American colonists in Lexington, Massachusetts, ended in bloodshed and ignited the American Revolution.

constitutional government, that is, a system in which people are guaranteed certain rights under a set of fair laws and policies. But this vague concept could be applied in a number of ways, democracy being but one of them. The Roman Republic in the second century B.C. and Britain in the 1700s, for example, were both constitutional governments. They both had laws that guaranteed many basic rights. But neither was a democracy.

When the American leaders issued the *Declaration of Independence* in 1776, making their split with Britain official, they were still unsure about what form their future government might take. So the document became no more than a statement of general principles. Its chief author, Thomas Jefferson, borrowed many ideas about liberty, equality, and government by the people from popular writers, especially Locke. "We hold these truths to be self-evident," Jefferson stated in the *Declaration:*

> that all men are created equal; that they are en-
> dowed by their Creator with certain unalienable
> rights; that among these are life, liberty, and the
> pursuit of happiness; that to secure these rights,
> governments are instituted among men, deriving
> their just powers from the consent of the gov-
> erned; that whenever any form of government be-
> comes destructive of these ends, it is the right of
> the people to alter or to abolish it, and to institute
> new government.

The document goes on to list British abuses against the colonies and concludes with the important statement of separation from the mother country.

Fear of the "great beast"

After the United States won its war of independence in 1781, American leaders faced the task of creating a government for the new country. Debates about how to do this were long and heated. Most of the founders desired a government based on democratic principles. But many were reluctant to commit to the radical kind of democracy

Thomas Jefferson puts the finishing touches on the Declaration of Independence, which Jefferson wrote almost entirely by himself.

Jefferson's original draft of the Declaration of Independence.

Rousseau had advocated, one in which all people in society have a direct and equal voice. Most American leaders were upper-class, wealthy landholders. They considered themselves more intelligent and better bred than the common people and therefore better able to govern. This superior attitude was a holdover from British society, which had a long history of upper-class aristocrats dominating society and government.

Many founders referred to the general public as a "great beast." They feared that a democracy that gave this beast too much direct power would be weak, chaotic, and eventually fail. One influential American aristocrat, Alexander Hamilton, summed up this opinion saying, "When the deliberative [decision-making] or judicial powers are vested wholly or partly in the collective body of the people, you must expect error, confusion and instability."

Hamilton also feared that if the wealthy gave up their hold on political power they might put themselves in danger. "Give all power to the many, they will oppress the few," he said. John Adams agreed, commenting, "The rich ought to have an effectual barrier in the constitution against being robbed, plundered, and murdered, as well as the poor." Clearly, the aristocrats worried that a direct democracy controlled by the people was too radical and dangerous. Thus, some degree of democracy was good but too much was bad.

A balance of power

But just as they feared too many people having power, the founders also feared too few having it. After all, the war of independence had begun as a protest against the tyranny of the British power elite—the king and Parliament. On this point, the founders agreed with Locke and

Colonial leader Alexander Hamilton believed that too democratic a government would not succeed.

The drafting committee presents the finished Declaration of Independence to the Continental Congress for signing on July 4, 1776.

Montesquieu. These writers had argued strongly that the powers of the lawmakers, the administrators, and the courts should be kept separate. That way, no one person or group could acquire too much power and become tyrannical. Jefferson summarized this view, saying that the new government should be one "in which the powers of government should be so divided and balanced among several bodies and magistracies [offices], as that no one could transcend their legal limits, without being effectively checked and restrained by the others."

The founders spelled out their solution to the problem of safely balancing power among the many and the few in a written federal constitution, completed in September 1787. This document granted executive powers to the president and vice president. It also provided for a legislative branch, the Congress, and a judicial branch, the Supreme Court.

Each branch would be independent of and have the authority to check the powers of the other two. For instance, Congress checks presidential power by having sole authority to make laws and to assign how the government's money will be used. By having the power to create rules for court procedures, the Congress also holds a check over the judiciary. The president's check on Congress is the power to veto, or reject, laws proposed by that body. The president influences the Supreme Court through his or her power to appoint judges. The Court holds checks over both the executive and legislative branches with its power to declare acts by these branches unconstitutional. In this way, the founders made sure that no single government branch would hold too much power.

The founders also structured the government to keep the people from having too much power. They did this in a number of ways. First, they did not call the new government a democracy, a term still primarily associated with the direct democracy of ancient Athens. The founders chose instead the term "representative republic." Founder

The nation's founders hammer out the details of the U.S. Constitution in 1787.

James Madison tried to explain the differences of the two systems:

> The two great points of difference between a democracy and a [representative] republic are: first, the delegation of the government, in the latter, to a small number of citizens elected by the rest; secondly, the greater number of citizens, and greater sphere of country, over which the latter may be extended.

Madison believed the creation of representative government was a practical necessity. Athens and the other Greek democracies had been small enough for direct democracy to work. But it was obviously impossible for hundreds of thousands or millions of Americans to regularly meet together, debate, and vote on issues. It was therefore necessary for the people to elect a small number of representatives to carry on the business of government.

However, the founders also felt that representation by a small number of citizens would ensure that society would continue to be controlled by its "best" people. Most American leaders sincerely believed that people like themselves would be the natural choice in elections. As writer Anthony Arblaster stated:

> The intention was that the electors [voters] should choose to be governed by persons they recognized as better and wiser than themselves, who might well understand better than the people themselves what their real interests were, and whose decisions the people would therefore accept. . . . A representative system of government, coupled with a division of powers, was thus seen as providing safeguards against the dangers of democracy.

Protecting the few from the many

The founders created two major safeguards to keep the masses from gaining and exercising too much power. The first was to limit the people's ability to elect members of Congress. The Constitution divided Congress into two parts—the House of Representatives and the Senate. House

The framers of the Constitution at Independence Hall in Philadelphia. The framers did not intend to create a democracy, but to protect the rights of every U.S. citizen.

members were elected by the people, as they are today. The number of House members from a given state depends on that state's population. As the state population increases, so does its representation in the House.

By contrast, the founders provided that each state would have two senators. These senators would be chosen by the state legislatures instead of the people. Because these legislatures were usually controlled by well-to-do landowners, they naturally chose people like themselves to be senators. It was the Senate's role to approve any law proposed and passed by the House before that law could become official. The founders also gave the Senate sole power to try and convict corrupt federal officials. With these sweeping powers, the Senate, a nonelected body, helped members of the upper classes maintain considerable control over the government.

Indirect election

Another safeguard against the masses acquiring too much power was the indirect, rather than direct, election of the president and vice president. The founders did not feel comfortable with the people voting directly for candidates to these chief executive offices. As a result, the Constitution also established the electoral college.

The electoral college consisted of delegates called electors who voted once every four years for the chief executives. The number of electors was equal to the total number of senators and House members. The state legislatures chose the electors, as they did senators. Because the people elected the members of the state legislatures, who chose the electors, who, in turn, chose the president, the people had only a small and indirect say in who ran the country. Popular presidential elections still took place but were essentially mean-

Andrew Jackson received a majority of popular votes in the 1824 presidential election but he did not become president because he did not receive the majority of electoral votes. In Jackson's time, electoral votes, not popular votes, determined presidential elections.

ingless. A candidate who received a majority of popular votes could lose the election to someone who received the most electoral votes. This happened in the 1824 election. Andrew Jackson won the popular vote but lost the election to John Quincy Adams, who won the electoral college's vote. This system was hardly democratic.

The original U.S. system contained another decidedly undemocratic feature. This was a very limited franchise, or right to vote. At first, only adult white males could vote and many of these were denied that right because of state and local property restrictions. Women and slaves could not vote at all. Thus, though the nation had been founded on the principle of equality, in practice few enjoyed equal rights. This situation was not surprising. Athens's enlightened direct democracy had similar voting limitations, as did Britain's parliamentary government in the 1600s and 1700s. Throughout history, wealthy, influential men dominated nearly all societies and governments, and the U.S. founders accepted this as the natural way of things.

An increasingly democratic system

The early United States had only a very limited kind of democracy. The system excluded large segments of the population from the political process and favored the participation of those with money, prestige, and influence. Yet the founders had laid the foundation for a more democratic system. They had created a strong Constitution with many safeguards against tyranny.

Even more important, the Constitution was flexible. The founders had provided for making changes and additions, called amendments, which could become law if ratified by three quarters of the state legislatures. With the use of such amendments, the system became increasingly democratic. For example, in 1791, only four years after the Constitution was signed, the government added ten amendments. Collectively known as the Bill of Rights, these ten amendments guaranteed several basic liberties that had not been spelled out in the original Constitution. The First Amendment, for example, states:

> Congress shall make no law respecting an establishment of religion, or prohibiting the free exercise thereof; or abridging [denying] the freedom of speech, or of the press; or the right of the people peaceably to assemble, and to petition the government for redress of grievances.

The Bill of Rights also guaranteed the rights to bear arms, to receive due process of law and a

Pioneers establish a homestead on the American frontier. The frontier experience gave rise to a more democratic interpretation of the U.S. Constitution.

speedy trial, and to be represented in court by defense counsel. By March 1971, the number of constitutional amendments had grown to twenty-six.

Another reason the U.S. government gradually became more democratic was that people's attitudes about society, government, and life in general changed. This led to new and often more democratic interpretations of the Constitution and laws. Unlike Britain, the United States was a new nation with an expanding frontier. Most Americans were fiercely independent and enterprising small farmers, merchants, and pioneers who took the nation's democratic principles at face value.

They did not see themselves as many of the founders did, as part of an inferior and dangerous mob.

As the years went on, increasing numbers of middle- and lower-class Americans demanded a greater voice in government. At the same time, the power, prestige, and influence of the wealthy landowners declined. In a sense, then, the government became more democratic because of pressures to satisfy the needs and desires of most of the people.

An inspiration for the world

As the nation put its democratic ideals into practice, the government's more undemocratic features fell away. For example, the workings of the electoral college eventually became a largely meaningless and traditional ceremony. After 1800, more and more states began choosing electors by popular elections, and today all states do so. In addition, today the electoral vote is tied directly to the popular vote. In an election, the candidate who receives the highest number of popular votes in a state automatically gets all of that state's electoral votes.

Other undemocratic practices disappeared as well. In 1913, the Seventeenth Amendment to the Constitution established the popular election of senators. Subsequently, all members of Congress were chosen by the people. Also, rules regulating citizenship and voting rights were expanded. By 1845, most restrictions to white males voting had been removed. In 1863, President Abraham Lincoln freed the black slaves in his Emancipation Proclamation, and the Thirteenth Amendment officially abolished slavery in 1865. In 1868 and 1870 respectively, the Fourteenth and Fifteenth Amendments granted American blacks citizenship and voting rights. And in 1920, the Nineteenth Amendment granted women the right to vote.

The U.S. founders did not foresee all of these dramatic changes. Their goal had been not to create a democracy, but to establish a fair constitutional government with selected democratic features. They succeeded in this goal and in the process produced something much greater. Their system was so fair, well-constructed, and flexible that it grew by degrees into the freest and strongest democracy in world history. The founders' great achievement, therefore, was the creation of a system that could grow to accommodate new and increasingly democratic ideas and practices.

Moreover, the American democratic experiment demonstrated that democracy could indeed work on a large scale. All through the 1800s and

President Abraham Lincoln and other officials sign the Emancipation Proclamation in 1863. Two years later, the Thirteenth Amendment to the Constitution abolished slavery in the United States, moving America one step closer to true democracy.

1900s, people across the globe studied U.S. democracy with interest and admiration. Perhaps no other unbiased observer offered as many insights into the American system as Alexis de Tocqueville. A French aristocrat, he toured the United States between 1831 and 1832. In his widely read and influential work *Democracy in America*, he wrote:

> The social condition of the Americans is eminently democratic. . . . Men are there seen on a greater equality in point of fortune and intellect, or, in other words, more equal in their strength, than in any other country of the world, or in any age of which history has preserved remembrance.

With each decade, the United States continues to expand and refine its democratic system. That system remains an inspiration to people everywhere who strive for freedom, equality, and the right to decide their own destinies.

Nineteenth-century French writer Alexis de Tocqueville's book Democracy in America *gave a glowing account of the American democratic system.*

4

The Influence of the French Revolution

THE AMERICAN REVOLUTION and establishment of the United States was the first of two great landmarks in the development of modern democracy. The second was the French Revolution, which began in 1789. In the decades before the revolution, France was a strict monarchy in which the king held supreme power. The royal family and noble classes, who made up only a tiny fraction of the population, lived in great luxury.

In contrast, most of the common people, comprising over 90 percent of the population, barely had enough to eat. Making matters worse, the poor commoners also carried most of the tax burden. Nobles and clergymen did not have to pay taxes on land. In addition, many of the country's laws unfairly favored the nobles and oppressed the commoners. Not surprisingly, frustration, anger, and a desire for reform grew among the French masses.

At the same time, more and more Frenchmen were inspired by the same writers and philosophers—Locke, Rousseau, and others—who had

(Opposite page) Armed French citizens liberate political prisoners from the Bastille on July 14, 1789. This action is still commemorated as the symbol of the liberation of the French people from absolute rulers.

influenced the Americans. These thinkers wrote about enlightened and fairer rights of human beings.

Influenced by such philosophical ideas, the French people eventually demanded social and legal equality for all citizens. The revolution they fought to gain this equality was turbulent and bloody. Although the rebellion did not end with the creation of a democratic state, as had happened in America, the French succeeded in eliminating most royal power over them. And their fight for liberty and basic human rights inspired other peoples in Europe and around the world to demand democratic reform in the decades that followed.

A bankrupt country

The chain of events leading to the French Revolution began in the early 1760s. At the time, France's economy was devastated when the country lost valuable North American lands and markets to Britain in the French and Indian War. Royal self-indulgence and financial mismanagement worsened the situation. King Louis XV, who died in 1774, wasted large sums of money on luxuries for his family, friends, and mistresses while his people starved. His successor, Louis XVI, was a well-meaning but poor ruler. During his reign, the national treasury continued to shrink until finally, in 1787, it was empty.

The only way Louis could raise the huge funds he needed to replenish the treasury was to levy heavy taxes on all French citizens, including the nobility. And the only legal way he could do this was to call a meeting of the States-General. This was the French version of medieval Europe's great councils that had met periodically to consider important matters of state. As France had grown into a strong monarchy in the 1400s and

Reforms in 1789 reduced the absolute monarchy of France's King Louis XVI to a constitutional monarchy.

1500s, the States-General had decreased in influence and importance. Its last meeting had taken place in 1614. Now in dire need of money, Louis called a new meeting of the States-General on May 5, 1789, in Versailles, near Paris. This move publicly demonstrated his desperation and weakened authority. It also raised many people's hopes that the king might finally be forced to consider his subjects' grievances. According to scholar R.K. Gooch in his book *Parliamentary Government in France:*

> The summoning of the States-General was a recognition of the fact that reform was imperative. It was also a recognition of the fact that the king could not, without the collaboration of the nation, effect real reform. . . . The king's acceptance, however reluctant, of the direction and force of public opinion aroused high hopes in the country.

Despite the fact that he was dealing from a position of weakness, Louis maintained a superior,

The reassembly of France's States-General in 1789. The seldom-used advisory body had not met for 175 years before Louis XVI reconvened it to ask for money.

arrogant attitude. Apparently, he expected the delegates of the States-General to automatically bow to his wishes and to vote to raise the funds he needed.

However, things did not go as Louis had planned. When the meeting began, arguments immediately erupted over voting procedures. The delegates were divided into three groups, each representing an estate, or class, of society. The clergy constituted the first estate, the nobles the second estate, and the commoners the third estate. According to tradition, each estate had a single, collective vote. But the members of the third estate objected to this arrangement. They argued that the privileged clergy and nobles would, as they had in the past, always vote together, two-to-one, against them. The commoners demanded that the rules be changed to give each and every delegate of the meeting a vote. Since the clergy had 308 delegates, the nobles 285, and the commoners 621, that would give the third estate a majority voice.

When the first two estates refused to change the voting rules, the members of the third angrily walked out of the meeting. Soon afterward, they held their own meeting on a nearby tennis court. Stating that they represented the wishes of most French citizens, they boldly declared themselves to be the National Assembly of France. They then took the famous "Oath of the Tennis Court," swearing never to disband until they had created a constitution for the country.

The desire for civil rights

At the time, the members of the new National Assembly did not intend to make France a democracy. Nor did they intend to eliminate the monarchy. They simply felt it was unfair that most French citizens did not have the same social

After walking out of the States-General convention, members of the Third Estate meet nearby at the king's tennis courts and declare themselves to be the French National Assembly.

and legal privileges enjoyed by a handful of aristocrats. The members of the third estate were content to remain under kingly rule as long as the king fairly extended them such privileges.

Among the middle and lower classes, desire for social and legal reform had been growing for decades. This desire was fueled by their frustration and anger over their miserable living conditions. The desire for reform was also greatly influenced by popular French writers and thinkers. The most influential of these were known as the Encyclopaedists because they all, at one time or another, contributed articles to a popular French

The satirical wit of the French writer Voltaire often angered the French government.

encyclopedia. Among them were Rousseau and Montesquieu. Others included Denis Diderot, Jean Le Rond d'Alembert, and Francois Marie Arouet, who wrote under the pen name of Voltaire.

Writers criticize the monarchy

Influenced by Locke, these writers championed basic human rights such as liberty and equality under the law. Voltaire, the most popular of the Encyclopaedists in France, argued that British society was far fairer than French society. Britain had a king, too, he said, but most British subjects enjoyed civil rights that the French king denied his own people. Voltaire declared:

> English legislation has succeeded in restoring to each individual his natural rights, of which nearly all monarchies have deprived him. These rights are: entire freedom of person and property; freedom to speak to the nation in his writings, to be judged in criminal cases by a jury of independent citizens, to be judged according to the precise terms of the law, and to profess peacefully the religion of his choice.

Voltaire repeatedly criticized the French monarchy and urged the idea of equal rights for all French citizens. The government became angry with him, and on several occasions he had to flee the country. Diderot and other Encyclopaedists often published their ideas in secret for fear of arrest.

Of all these writers, Rousseau was unique in advocating true democracy. The others argued for the less ambitious, less radical goal of instituting fairer laws and social policies under the monarchy. The members of the National Assembly adopted this goal when they met on the tennis court. They hoped to draft a written constitution that would guarantee all French citizens basic civil rights, and then have Louis agree to and sign the document. In the following weeks, people all over France waited anxiously for word about the Assembly and the constitution.

The people's hopes were soon dashed, however. Rumors spread that the king planned to disband the National Assembly and thereby suppress the new civil rights movement. On July 14, 1789, the people of Paris rose in violent protest. An angry mob stormed the Bastille, a fortress-prison in which many of the government's political prisoners suffered for months, sometimes even years, without trials. When French troops received the order to fire on the rioters, they refused and joined the crowd. The mob then broke into the Bastille, killed the guards, and released the prisoners. Ever since, July 14 has been called "Bastille Day" and celebrated as France's independence day.

A declaration of rights

Following the Bastille's fall, similar uprisings and demonstrations against the government occurred in other parts of the country. Emboldened by the courage of the French masses, on August 26

An angry mob of peasants marches in the French countryside during nationwide riots in 1789.

The Bastille is taken over by rioting civilians. With the fall of this fortress-prison the French Revolution began in earnest.

the National Assembly issued its *Declaration of the Rights of Man and of the Citizen*. The declaration was intended as the first section of the new constitution. "The representatives of the people of France," the document began:

> formed into a National Assembly, considering that ignorance, neglect, or contempt of human rights, are the sole causes of public misfortunes and corruptions of government, have resolved to set forth in a solemn declaration these natural . . . and inalienable rights, that this declaration being constantly present to the minds of the members of the body social [society], they may be ever kept attentive to their rights and their duties . . . and also that future claims of the citizens, being directed by simple and incontestable [universally accepted] principles, may always tend to the maintenance of the Constitution and the general happiness. For these reasons the National Assembly doth recognize and declare, in the presence of the Supreme Being, and with the hope of His blessing and favor, the following sacred rights of men and of citizens.

The Declaration went on to list basic civil rights. Each stirring phrase echoed the sentiments of Locke and other great thinkers. Article III, for instance, stated that governmental power is derived from the people:

> The nation [meaning the people] is essentially the source of all sovereignty; nor can any individual, or any body of men, be entitled to any authority which is not expressly derived from it.

Like the American Bill of Rights, the French Declaration established specific civil liberties, including the right to be presumed innocent until proven guilty, freedom to hold and voice one's opinion, and freedom of religion.

The fall of the monarchy

Despite their statements about popular sovereignty, the members of the Assembly still found the traditional political system of monarchy acceptable. Hoping for Louis's approval, they presented the Declaration to him on October 2, 1789. As R.K. Gooch explains:

> Three days later, the president [of the Assembly] read to the Assembly the reply of the king. In a statement that dealt for the most part with other matters, the king at the end asserted that he would not concern himself at length with the Declaration of Rights. "It contains," he said, "some very good maxims [principles] well calculated to guide your labors." He then concluded: "But it includes principles susceptible to explanation and even of different interpretation, which can be justly appreciated only at the moment that their true sense is fixed by the statutes [laws] for which the declaration will serve as a foundation."

Thus, although Louis had not totally rejected the document, he had arrogantly stalled judgment on it until a later, unspecified time. Many people were disappointed and angry over the king's refusal to accept the Declaration. On October 5, a mob of women broke into the royal palace in

A solemn depiction of the French Declaration of the Rights of Man and of the Citizen, *drawn up by the National Assembly and presented to King Louis on October 2, 1789.*

Angered by the king's casual response to the Declaration of Rights, a group of women storms his palace to demand reforms.

Versailles, and from that time on, the Assembly had to assign guards to protect the king and his family.

The royal family remained under guard for more than a year while the Assembly finished drafting the new constitution. According to the new document, France was to be a constitutional monarchy. The king would be head of state but would have to answer to a national legislature. He would be unable to declare war, make peace, or perform many other important acts without the approval of the legislature. In September 1791, the Assembly disbanded itself to make way for the new legislature, which first convened on October 1.

The "Reign of Terror"

The events of the following years were chaotic and bloody. The legislature's most radical members, some of them violent, power-hungry men, gained control of the government. In April 1792, France went to war with two powerful European countries—Prussia and Austria. During the conflict, the king continued to refuse to accept the new government. Eventually, many people suspected him and the queen of plotting with enemy rulers to betray France. In August 1792, the legislature stripped the king of his powers and imprisoned him. The French monarchy was at an end.

With the king gone, government leaders declared France a republic and tried to redirect public loyalties to the state itself. They strongly promoted the idea of national patriotism. Everyone was expected to support the ideas and goals of the revolution. Those who did not were persecuted. As scholar Roy C. Macridis tells it:

> With the . . . overthrow of the monarchy in 1792, the French Revolution quickly established patrio-

tism as the highest ideal. Rituals, national festivals . . . and national songs were all used to create solidarity among the French. A system of national education was instituted to propagate patriotic values. . . . The republic was to be "one and indivisible." Compliance with the revolution and its policies was promoted everywhere, requiring coercive measures [force] that gradually were transformed into an outright tyranny.

Radical members of the legislature seemed to abandon the democratic ideals that had initiated the Revolution. France became a police state. Beginning early in 1793, the country endured what became known as the "Reign of Terror." The king, his family, and many other nobles were publicly beheaded. Anyone who seemed sympathetic to the monarchy or who was suspected of being against the new government met a similar fate.

Eventually, the radicals turned on each other, and moderates gained control of the government. But France was in a state of chaos. In 1799, a powerful army officer named Napoleon Bona-

A group of doomed political prisoners awaits execution during France's Reign of Terror.

Napoleon sought to bring order to the chaos following the French Revolution by installing himself as dictator. Many of his political reforms were retained after he was forced from power.

parte took advantage of the situation. He seized control of the government, claiming he was "restoring order," and made himself dictator.

The Revolution's ideals live on

In a few short years, France had evolved from monarchy to constitutional monarchy to constitutional republic to near anarchy and finally to military dictatorship. In the short run the Revolution had failed to bring a democratic government to France. But in the long run, this great event significantly affected the rise of modern democracy because its ideals lived on.

France itself later reaffirmed democratic ideals when it established its Second Republic, with a representative parliament, in 1848. Under subsequent French governments—the Third Republic

(1871), the Fourth Republic (1945), and the Fifth Republic (1958)—the country became increasingly democratic. For example, French women gained voting rights in 1945. And in 1958 the French president gained executive powers similar to those of the U.S. presidents.

During all of these years, the original French *Declaration of the Rights of Man* remained the guiding force in creating government and framing laws. Thus, those who struggled and died in the Revolution left behind a legacy that helped France evolve into one of the world's great democracies.

The legacy of the French Revolution also had an impact on the political systems of other countries. During the 1800s, the ideals of liberty, social equality, and popular participation in government swept through Europe and other parts of the

Members of the French senate are elected by the National Assembly.

The emblem of the French Revolution declares that the reformers seek either democratic principles—unity, the indivisibility of the republic, liberty, equality, and fraternity—or death.

world. According to Anthony Arblaster, the French people's bold bid for political power over their king:

> transformed the modern history of democracy. At a stroke, we might almost say, political ideas which had only been aspirations or dreams in the minds of [philosophers] and popular radicals, were placed on the agenda of real politics, not only in France or even Europe, but globally. The principles and example of the Revolution helped to inspire the first successful slave revolt in the Caribbean [Sea] in Haiti, as well as the political independence movements of South America. All such movements raised the issue of democracy, of popular power.

Historian J.L. Talmon commented on the Revolution's global influence when he wrote:

> The Declaration of 1789 had solemnly proclaimed the right to oppose oppression, indeed, enunciated [spelled out] the duty to resist it. . . . The French Revolution had proclaimed the rights of man and promised equality. And from then onwards . . . any injury to what came to be thought of as the dignity of man, began to appear as intolerable, and justifying resistance.

The spirit of resistance to oppression grew into a revolutionary fervor that finally exploded in 1848. When the French created the Second Republic and reestablished their revolutionary ideals, they ignited a political firestorm. Uprisings occurred all over the continent. The Austrian people forced their emperor off his throne, and his successor had to adopt fairer, more liberal political policies. In Hungary, the people demanded and won a new constitution that recognized several basic human rights. And demands for political reform echoed through Italy, Germany, and other nations.

At the time, none of these countries completely discarded their old systems and became democracies. Yet the ideas of liberty, social equality, and

Though it took centuries for France to achieve its revolutionary ideals, its example inspired many other European nations to fight for democracy. This drawing depicts the uprising of the Austrian people in 1848.

popular government had taken firm root in Europe. In time, after numerous wars, revolutions, and political struggles, democratic systems would become the rule there.

Thus, the legacy of the French Revolution was, in its simplest terms, the spirit of political reform. That spirit proved to be compelling and unstoppable. The desperate cries of Paris's downtrodden for "Liberty! Equality! Fraternity!" captured the minds and hearts of millions and eventually transformed the world.

5

Britain and Parliamentary Democracy

THE FRENCH REVOLUTION encouraged the ideas of liberty and social equality in Europe in the late 1700s and early 1800s. But the revolutionaries had not created a stable or lasting form of government based on their ideals. Therefore, while the French inspired others to institute democratic reform, they did not provide a working model of a modern democracy.

On the other side of the Atlantic Ocean, however, the United States had established a government by the people. But at that time, most Europeans viewed the United States as remote from European affairs. Its government seemed to be the result of a unique set of circumstances, and many people believed the American experiment would eventually prove unworkable. So at first, few looked at the U.S. government as a model to copy.

Both the French and Americans had derived most of their democratic ideas from Britain's longstanding parliamentary system. By the time of the French Revolution, the British had evolved

(Opposite page) A drawing of the English Parliament in the fourteenth century. British parliamentary democracy has served as a model for most of the democracies in the world today.

a workable representative government. It was far from being a democracy. Yet it was also far ahead of all other nations, except the United States, in guaranteeing its people basic civil liberties. After all, the American Revolution had begun as an attempt to maintain these very liberties.

The British system was also flexible and therefore subject to democratic change. Such change, in fact, had been going on in Britain for hundreds of years and it continued throughout the nineteenth century. "The resulting system of parliamentary democracy," explains political scientist Frederick M. Watkins,

> was quite different from but no less successful than the American system. Except in South and Central America, where democratic constitutions generally tended, as in the United States, to follow the presidential pattern, Britain was almost everywhere taken as the model of modern constitutional democracy, no country in history being thus so widely imitated.

Today, most of the world's democracies have parliamentary systems similar to Britain's.

A flexible constitution

Without doubt, the backbone of the British system is its strong constitution. This liberal constitution was the starting point for the differing explorations of democratic ideas by Locke, Voltaire, and Jefferson. Yet in one sense, calling Britain a constitutional democracy is somewhat misleading. This is because the country is one of the few in the world that does not have a *written* constitution. Strathearn Gordon writes:

> Before me lies open a copy of "The Constitution of the United States of America," starting with the words: "We, the people . . . in order to form a more perfect union . . . do ordain and establish this CONSTITUTION. . . ." It runs to sixteen small pages and can be purchased anywhere in America.

The seals of King John from the Magna Carta, one of the documents that serves to limit the power of the British government.

If you ask for the address of a shop where you can buy a copy of the British Constitution, the answer is that no such document exists. . . . It is described and discussed in countless textbooks, but no one [in Britain] has ever sat down . . . to "ordain and establish" a Constitution, as did fifty-five American delegates in 1787.

Of what, then, does the British constitution consist? First, it is a collection of various laws passed by Parliament over the course of centuries. It is also a collection of diverse documents, such as the Magna Carta, English Bill of Rights, and Parliament Act of 1911, each limiting the government's power in some way. The British constitution also consists of certain customs and practices that the British have developed over the years. Many of these practices, such as choosing the country's leader, are not specified anywhere in writing. Instead, political leaders are expected to follow these customs and practices on a kind of honor system. This differs sharply with the U.S. system, in which the limits and rules of governmental power are all set down precisely in writing.

Because Britain's constitution is a varied collection of laws, documents, ideas, and customs accumulated over centuries, it is very flexible. Parliament can change a part of it at any time simply by passing a new act. The constitution will also change if most of the people come to accept a new political idea or practice. By contrast, changing America's written constitution requires considerable time, effort, and legal procedures. Because of its extraordinary flexibility, the British constitution has allowed democratic ideas and institutions to evolve steadily in Britain over the centuries.

The growth and triumph of Parliament

Democratic ideas and institutions developed in late medieval times in Britain and immediately limited the king's power. While most other Euro-

England's King Charles I refused to obey limitations placed on him by Parliament in 1629.

pean nations were developing into absolute monarchies, the British monarchy was steadily weakening. This weakened power was largely due to the rapid growth of Parliament and the checks placed on kingly power.

After King Edward I created the Model Parliament in 1295, representative government developed quickly. At first, the representatives of the nobles and the commoners met together. Then in the mid-1300s they began meeting separately. Ever since, Britain's Parliament has been divided into the House of Lords, called the Lords, and the House of Commons, called the Commons.

Not surprisingly, the Lords originally had the most power. But the power of the Commons grew steadily. By the mid-1400s, they had gained the rights to review tax legislation and introduce new laws. During the following two centuries, Parliament placed more and more limits on the monarch's power to do these things. And all the while, because Parliament operated by open debate, the right of free speech and other civil liberties became the custom of the land, and therefore part of the evolving constitution.

Civil war erupts

In time, the country's kings and queens grew bitter about their loss of power. In 1629, King Charles I challenged Parliament and refused to obey new rules limiting his powers. This led to civil war in the 1640s between the supporters of Charles and those of Parliament. Parliament won, however, and had the king beheaded in 1649. This was not an attempt to end the monarchy, but to make it clear that the king could not do as he pleased. He must obey the country's accumulated laws and customs, that is, its constitution.

After that, Parliament's power grew even faster. In 1689, it issued the English Bill of

Forces of King Charles I battle those of Parliament during the seventeenth-century British civil war.

Rights which firmly established its effective dominance over the monarchy. According to scholar Anthony H. Birch, the Bill:

> declared, among other things, that henceforth the monarch could neither make nor suspend laws without the consent of Parliament; that he could not raise money except by parliamentary grant [permission]; that he could not maintain a standing army without parliamentary authority; and that neither he nor anyone else could restrict the right of free speech within Parliament.

Perhaps the Bill's most important provision was the one that forbade the king from raising money

Before their coronation in 1689, the British king and queen, William and Mary, ratified the new Bill of Rights.

without Parliament's approval. Holding the country's purse strings, Parliament was clearly in charge.

Democracy by degrees

Thus, by the early 1700s Britain had a partially democratic system of political representation, many basic civil rights, and a monarchy that bowed to the wishes of the legislature. The country also had a flexible constitution that had become more and more democratic with time. It was perhaps inevitable, then, that the British system would eventually evolve into a democracy.

A number of influential British philosophers and political writers of the 1700s and 1800s urged various social, political, and economic reforms. Their ideas dramatically stimulated the ongoing evolution of Britain's democratic institutions.

In his 1789 work *Introduction to Principles of Morals and Legislation*, philosopher Jeremy Bentham argued that the object of government should be to bring people happiness. "The greatest happiness of the greatest number is the foundation of morals and legislation," he wrote. According to Bentham, the best way to assure people's happiness is to allow them complete civil liberties such as freedom of expression and religion. And democracy is the political system that most effectively allows for civil liberties.

Rights of the individual

In the 1800s, John Stuart Mill supported and expanded Bentham's arguments. Mill believed that democracy was the preferable form of government because it would raise the quality of life for everyone. Democracy could do this by providing freedom from social as well as political oppression. To Mill, social liberty meant equality

Eighteenth-century English political philosopher Jeremy Bentham wrote that the object of government was to make people happy by granting them civil liberties.

Nineteenth-century English philosopher John Stuart Mill championed equality—for women as well as men—as the foundation of democracy.

under the law, the freedom of privacy, and the right to think and express one's own opinions. "The principle of democracy," Mill stated in his 1861 work *Considerations on Representative Government*, "professes equality as its very root and foundation."

In championing the democratic rights of the individual, Mill also advocated equality and civil rights for women. He argued that it is unfair to define "the individual" in the political and legal sense as being strictly male. Women are individuals, too, he said, and deserve the same rights as men, including the right to vote.

Influenced by Bentham, Mill, and other writers and thinkers, British legislators introduced many democratic reforms in the 1800s and early 1900s. They did not need to resort to violent revolution, as the French had. A parliamentary system was already in place in Britain, and the reformers needed only to concentrate on gaining more control of Parliament.

A strong and fair democracy

As the reformers gained control over the course of decades, the government steadily developed into a full-fledged democracy. The Reform Act of 1832 expanded voting rights for men. The Act also increased the power and prestige of the Commons, which gave the voice of everyday people more weight in the government. Legislation in 1867, 1884, and 1918 further expanded male voting rights, and in 1928 British women received full voting rights.

The Parliamentary Act of 1911 was particularly important. It greatly reduced the powers of the Lords, and from that time on, the Commons controlled the government. Thus, by the early twentieth century, all adult British citizens could vote and the government rested firmly in the hands of the people. In this way, Britain, like the United States, became a strong and fair democracy by degrees.

Absolute majority rule

Despite their similar democratic evolutions, Britain and the United States developed distinctly different democratic systems. For example, in the United States the executive and legislative branches of government are separate; the president and Congress represent two different

An English suffragist demands voting rights for women in Great Britain in 1912. British women were given the right to vote in 1928.

The halls of the British House of Commons. The Commons has gradually become the more powerful house in the British Parliament.

branches of government. By contrast, in Britain, the executive and legislative branches of government are combined in one government body called Parliament.

The British Parliament is made up of "Members of Parliament," or MPs. Members of the House of Commons are chosen in a general national election, while most members of the House of Lords inherit their seats from relatives. The Commons' function is to make laws and determine how the country is run. The House of Lords, mainly an advisory body, reviews and occasionally changes or adds to proposed legislation. The country's chief executive is the prime minister. He or she is the leader of the political party that holds the most seats in the Commons and is selected by members of the majority party. The prime minister chooses members of his or her own party, forming a cabinet of lesser ministers to help run the country. Therefore, the nation's top executives are also members of the legislature. The minority party in Parliament is known as the "loyal Opposition."

The prime minister and his or her cabinet are usually referred to as the "Government." They draw up legislative bills and introduce them to Parliament. The Government and Opposition then debate the bills in the Commons. Since the Government is part of the majority party, most bills have a good chance of passing. Occasionally, however, the Commons votes against the Government on an important issue, thereby giving the Government a "vote of no confidence." When this happens, the prime minister and the cabinet usually resign and a new election is held. Often, the Opposition wins the election and its leader becomes prime minister.

Another important difference between the U.S. and British systems is the way each sets limits on governmental power. In the United States, the written constitution provides for specific legal checks and balances among the various branches. By contrast, in Britain, the leaders of the majority party have practically unlimited powers as long as they enjoy the confidence and political support of the people. What, then, keeps these leaders from abusing their power? The simplest answer is that the people trust them to act in a decent, moral manner, to uphold the democratic traditions that make up the constitution. Frederick Watkins explains:

> The constitutional tradition of Britain . . . is conceived in moral rather than legal terms. Most Englishmen would agree that a majority, acting through proper parliamentary channels, has a legal right to do anything it wishes, but would also agree that there are many things a majority has no moral right to do, and that if those things were attempted, even by act of Parliament, they would still be in violation of the principles of the constitution. Civil liberties, for example, are at least as secure in England as in any other country, not because they are legally guaranteed . . . but because the tradition of respect for British liberties is so widely shared that it would be morally unthinkable for a majority to violate them.

Therefore, when they elect leaders, British voters desire and fully expect those leaders to have whatever power is necessary to carry out the people's wishes. And the only major restraint on that power is adherence to constitutional traditions. No other nation has gone as far as Britain in enacting the principle of absolute majority rule.

The British model

Britain's parliamentary democracy did more than fulfill the needs of the British people. It also acted as a model for other countries. During the nineteenth and twentieth centuries, many European nations followed the same general pattern as

Britain. They gradually replaced their monarchies with parliamentary governments that derive their powers from a majority of the people. One example is France.

Although the spirit of reform in France was driven by the ideals of the French Revolution, when the French finally established a democratic government, they copied the British model. By the late 1800s, the French parliamentary system was firmly in place. And by the 1920s, most other European countries had parliaments similar to Britain's. Many nations in other parts of the world also followed Britain's lead. Canada, Australia, New Zealand, and India are among the many countries that developed parliamentary governments.

These governments differ from Britain's on one major point. They all have written constitutions. These documents describe the structure and

Members of the French parliament elect their president. Unlike Britain's Parliament, on which it is based, the French government follows a written constitution.

powers of government and impose certain legal restrictions on the parliamentary majority. In this respect, these countries chose to follow the U.S. model, which relies on a strong written constitution to limit government power. In nearly all other ways, however, parliamentary governments follow Britain's example.

But Britain has supplied more than a model for the structure of democratic government. Through its gradual evolution of a fair and liberal political tradition, the country has played a crucial role in the development of modern democracy. The British effectively curbed their monarchy's power and developed political representation and basic civil liberties. They also produced thinkers like Locke, who advocated popular government. These events and ideas eventually inspired the American and French revolutions, which, in turn, spearheaded the drive for democracy around the world. Thus, just as ancient democracy sprang from the Athenian experiment, modern democracy owes much to the British.

6

Democracy in a Rapidly Changing World

THE TWENTIETH CENTURY has been a time of rapid, dramatic, and sometimes catastrophic change on a scale unprecedented in world history. Over fifty million people died in World War II. During and after that terrible conflict, whole nations collapsed while others came into being. Meanwhile, technological and social changes transformed people's lives. Radio and television brought world events into people's living rooms. Air travel, widespread industrialization, and computers became necessary elements of a global economy, in which each nation depends for its well-being on many others.

While these transformations occurred, political systems changed, too. Democratic government became more attractive, and the number of democracies in the world grew rapidly. When the twentieth century began, fewer than a dozen democracies existed. By 1980, the number had grown to at least fifty-six. Many people, especially those who lived in the democracies, saw this trend as positive and hopeful. It seemed to

(Opposite page) The statue of Vladimir Lenin, founder of Soviet communism, is removed from the town square of Bucharest, Romania, in 1990. Romania and other Eastern European nations greeted the last decade of the twentieth century by trying to replace communist dictatorships with democracies.

97

them that, politically speaking, the complete democratization of the world was inevitable. The fall of communism in many European countries in the early 1990s seemed to strengthen this argument.

When the Soviet Union broke up into many smaller states, most of them professed a desire to become democratic. For many people around the world, this confirmed that undemocratic, dictatorial systems are unworkable and outmoded and that democracy is the wave of the future.

But some people question whether global democracy is possible. They claim that the many military, economic, and social problems in various parts of the world make total democratization difficult. They also point out that democracy appears to be failing in some nations and that the

Jubilant Czechoslovakians cheer the announcement of a new, democratic government in late 1989.

number of democracies could easily decrease over time. Perhaps, they say, democracy works for some peoples and nations but not for others. According to this view, the world is changing so quickly and so unpredictably that global politics may be drastically different in the next century than it is now. Therefore, the future of democracy, as well as other political systems, must remain an open question.

A dramatic success story

Regardless of how many nations eventually become democratic, the growth and success of democracy in the twentieth century has certainly been remarkable. This is partly due to the promotion and defense of freedom by the great democracies—the United States, Britain, and France. In World War II these countries banded together as allies against the threat of world conquest by the German Nazis and the Japanese. After winning the war, the Allies transformed their former enemies into democratic states, which became models for many other countries around the world. According to political scientist D.A. Rustow:

> The Allied victory in the Second World War removed the threat of Nazi tyranny and Japanese military conquest. American occupation policies in West Germany and Japan made a major contribution to the global spread of democracy.

Germany and Japan had been two of the most undemocratic countries in the world. Under dictatorships, these nations had brought about the century's greatest political upheavals. Yet after the war, they underwent a dramatic change from dictatorial to democratic government and became peaceful, successful, and prosperous societies. If democracy could work so well in these nations, many people argued, it could certainly work elsewhere.

A nineteenth-century Japanese knight (on horseback) and a foot soldier. Within the space of a century Japan's feudalistic dictatorship gave way to a modern democracy.

Japan's success story was particularly dramatic. The country did not have a strong historical tradition of democratic ideas and institutions as western European nations had. As late as the mid-1800s, Japan was still an authoritarian, feudal system controlled by emperors and powerful warlords. It was isolated from the rest of the world, as well as economically and militarily backward. To correct this situation, the Japanese successfully established a massive economic and social modernization program in the late 1800s and early 1900s. But political change did not keep pace with other reforms. Japan rejected Western democratic ideas, became an aggressive, warlike state, and eventually threatened the world.

Considering Japan's history, many people were amazed that the Japanese strongly embraced Western ways, including democracy, after World War II. For a nation that had no real understanding of or experience with democratic institutions, the Japanese adapted quickly to their new political system. They now had a parliament, called the Diet, a prime minister, and free elections. They also had a new constitution, which officially went into effect in 1947.

"We, the Japanese people," the document begins:

> acting through our duly elected representatives in the National Diet, determined that we shall secure for ourselves and our posterity the fruits of peaceful cooperation with all nations and the blessings of liberty throughout this land, and resolved that never again shall we be visited with the horrors of war through the action of government, do proclaim that sovereign power resides with the people and do firmly establish this Constitution.

Making democracy work

In many ways, the Japanese constitution is similar to the U.S. Bill of Rights and the constitutions of other democracies. It guarantees basic

In 1946, members of Japan's parliament, called the Diet, bow as Emperor Hirohito announces Japan's new constitution.

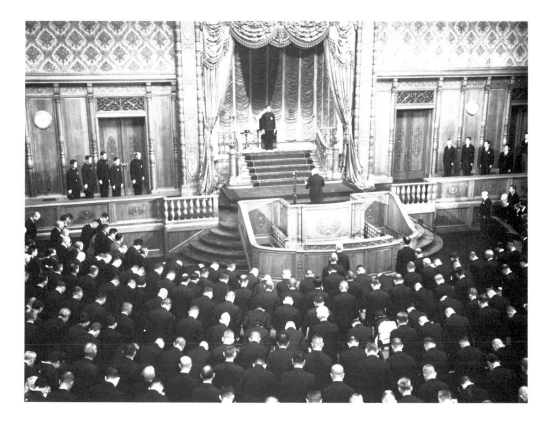

civil rights and provides for a fair judiciary system. However, the Japanese constitution is unique among those of the modern democracies in that it specifically renounces war. Article Nine states:

> Aspiring sincerely to an international peace based on justice and order, the Japanese people forever renounce war as a sovereign right of the nation and the threat or use of force as a means of settling international disputes.

To accomplish this aim, the Japanese maintain no large offensive land or sea forces. And in this may lie one of the key reasons for the success of Japan's democratic system. The country has not had to spend large sums on its military, as the United States and other democracies have. So Japan has been able to invest a large proportion of its money in business, commercial, and technological enterprises. This factor, along with the Japanese people's ingenuity and hard work, has made the country an economic giant. In the 1980s, Japan had the highest rate of economic growth of all the world's industrialized countries. This remarkable economic success has convinced the Japanese that democracy works and thus strength-

Steve Kelley/Copley News Service. Reprinted with permission.

ened their commitment to democratic institutions. It is no wonder that the United States, Britain, and others often referred to the Japanese example when promoting democracy after World War II.

In the years following World War II, the large democracies saw much fertile ground in which to plant the seeds of democracy. The war's huge upheavals had displaced whole populations and redrawn national borders. Over time this led to the creation of many new countries. In 1945, the newly created United Nations organization had a membership of 50 nations. By the late 1970s, that membership had grown to more than 150. Of the dozens of fledgling nations that opted for democratic government, most, like Japan, copied the British model and established parliamentary systems.

A host of problems

The number of democracies in the world continued to grow during the post-war era. Today there are more democracies than ever before. A 1992 survey conducted by Freedom House, a U.S. human rights group, examined the political systems of 186 countries. The survey showed 75 countries to be genuine democracies. The survey also showed another 38 countries to be "repressive," meaning that they deny basic freedoms, human rights, and popular government. The other 73 countries were judged partially free. In a way, this survey had good news for supporters of democracy. Not only are there more democracies than repressive regimes, but the number of democracies grew by over 25 percent during the 1980s. According to Freedom House executive director Bruce McColm, "The world is undeniably freer than it was a decade ago."

It is quite possible that the number of democracies throughout the world may continue to grow.

Spurred by the wave of democracy that passed through Eastern Europe and the Soviet Union in 1990, a sea of protestors fills the square in front of Taiwan's Chiang Kai-Shek Memorial, demanding a greater say in their government.

Several countries are presently in a state of transition and hope to form democratic governments by the mid-1990s. Among these are El Salvador in Central America, Ethiopia in Africa, Taiwan in Asia, and many of the former Soviet states.

Many people question whether democracy will be effective in these societies. They point out that a host of legal, social, economic, and other kinds of problems in these nations may keep their peoples from easily adapting to democracy the way the Japanese did. Stanford University political and foreign policy researcher Larry Diamond says:

> Many of these new "democracies" have initiated only the rudiments of democratic institutions. Elected executives lack effective control over the military and may need to weigh [political and social] actions against the threat of a coup [military takeover]. Legislatures are weak, poorly financed,

and understaffed. Legal systems lack the training, resources, and authority to protect human rights and due process. Political parties lack organization, resources . . . and the political skill and experience to govern effectively. Also missing, typically, is the cultural and civic infrastructure of democracy: a strong commitment to democracy widely shared [among all social groups] . . . and an independent . . . mass media.

The predicament that the former Soviets find themselves in is a clear example. These peoples presently face severe economic problems that threaten the growth of democracy. They also lack democratic political and legal experience. In April 1993, the Russians gave their new president, Boris Yeltsin—a strong advocate of democracy—a vote of confidence at the polls. But many political analysts say Yeltsin faces an uphill battle. They say that establishing an effective, workable democracy in Russia, if it happens at all, may take many years.

Some of the countries that have already made the transition to democracy in the last twenty years have suffered significantly from problems similar to those experienced in Russia. Of forty nations that have become democratic since 1973, about a third have experienced either a complete breakdown of democracy or a serious suppression

A Russian voter casts his ballot in one of the first elections in his country's history.

A protestor in New Delhi, India, is arrested by police during a 1993 demonstration. Government corruption and abuses of civil rights have seriously threatened India's democracy.

of civil rights and due process of law. Among these countries are Colombia, Pakistan, and Sri Lanka. Government abuses and corruption in India, the world's most populous democracy, prompted Freedom House to downgrade that country to a "partially free" status in 1992.

Many other nations are threatened by economic crisis. In several Latin American countries, for instance, incomes have dropped so low that many people are losing faith in their governments. Larry Diamond warns, "Many constitutional [democratic] regimes in Asia, Africa, Eastern Europe, and Latin America may collapse in this decade if they are not able to cope with economic and social changes." Freedom House's McColm agrees, saying, "Unless the community of democratic countries is aggressive in consolidating [its] gains, I fear we could see a downward trend in the rest of the 1990s."

Promoting democracy

Clearly, the international democratic community is worried that a downward trend in democracy will discourage its growth. The successful democracies feel they have good reasons for vigorously promoting democratic systems. First, they say, such a system is beneficial for the people who adopt it. The people have the right of free expression and the opportunity to have a voice in determining their own destinies. In general, less social and legal injustice, censorship, and political repression exists in democracies than in other systems.

Advocates of democracy say their system is also beneficial to the world community. "Democratic countries do not go to war with one another," U.S. president Bill Clinton said in 1992. "They don't sponsor terrorism or threaten one another with weapons of mass destruction." Indeed,

Former Canadian prime minister Brian Mulroney speaks at the 1993 U.S.-Russian economic summit meeting in Canada. The United States and Canada advocate giving the former Soviet republics economic aid to help them become democracies.

the case of the Soviet states renouncing communism and moving toward democracy shows how democracy might create a safer world. According to Larry Diamond:

> No region of the world better demonstrates urgent U.S. security interests in democratization than the former Soviet Union. If Russia, Ukraine, Kazakhstan, and other former Soviet states succeed in institutionalizing democracy, their military threat to Europe, Japan, and the United States will end, and they will become lasting partners in the search for global order and peace.

What should the United States and other democracies do to promote and strengthen democracy in the world? President Clinton and the leaders of other large democratic countries, such as Britain and Canada, advocate substantial

Former First Lady Eleanor Roosevelt displays the United Nations Declaration of Human Rights issued in 1948.

economic aid. Providing aid to these countries, they argue, is in the interests of all involved. D.A. Rustow summarizes this view:

> Since most new democracies of the late twentieth century were established in the wake of major economic failures by the preceding communist or military regimes, one of the first needs is for economic advice, investment and aid, for which there is a well-established . . . network, such as the International Monetary Fund and the World Bank, and private consultants.

Rustow also states it is important to provide technical information. For instance, after the collapse of the Soviet Union, U.S. officials advised their Russian counterparts on how to run a presidential office. "Generally," Rustow says, "the most useful service that the liberal democracies . . . can provide to the world's struggling democracies would seem to be the exchange of such technical information."

Enduring principles

Although the leaders of the free world are hopeful about continued democratization, democracy's future remains uncertain. It is likely that in the next century and the one that follows, many countries will cease to exist and new ones will be born. No one can predict the economic or other conditions these nations will face or the political systems they will embrace. But there is a glimmer of hope for the world's democrats.

In 1948, the United Nations issued its *Universal Declaration of Human Rights*. This document states the basic ideals and civil liberties that the United Nations hoped all countries would adopt. Echoing the stirring and enduring principles of the French and American revolutions, the U.N. document declared, among other things, that:

> All human beings are born free and equal in dignity and rights. They are endowed with reason and conscience and should act towards one another in a spirit of brotherhood. . . . Everyone has the right of life, liberty, and security of person. . . . Everyone has the right to recognition everywhere as a person before the law. . . . Everyone has the right to freedom of thought, conscience, and religion.

The question is whether or not the U.N. and strong democratic countries such as the United States and Britain will continue to vigorously promote the ideals stated in the U.N. document. If they do, the system that the Greeks introduced to the world so long ago will likely remain an attractive political alternative.

Appendix
Great Democratic Documents

THE MAGNA CARTA

In signing the Magna Carta in 1215, King John granted his English lords several guarantees of fair and consistent treatment by the king. This document is considered the foundation of all the English liberties and democratic principles that came later. Some of the Magna Carta's guarantees were:

We [the king] have granted . . . and given to all the Freemen of our realm, for us and our heirs forever, those liberties underwritten; to have and to hold, to them and their heirs for ever. . . .

The city of London shall have all the old liberties and customs which it hath been used to have. Moreover, we will and grant that all other cities and boroughs, towns, and the Barons of the Five Ports, and all other ports, shall have all their liberties and free customs. . . .

No constable [law officer], or other bailiff of ours, shall take corn or other chattels of any man, unless he presently gives him money for it. . . .

No sheriff or bailiff of ours, or any other, shall take horses or carts of any Freeman for transportation, unless with the consent of that freeman. . . .

No bailiff shall, upon his own unsupported complaint, put anyone to his "law," without credible witnesses brought for this purpose.

No Freeman shall be taken, or imprisoned, or disseised [deprived] of his freehold [property], or liberties, or free customs, or be outlawed, or exiled, or any otherwise destroyed, nor will we pass upon him, nor condemn him, but by lawful judgment of his peers, or by the law of the land. We will sell to no man, we will not deny or defer to any man, either justice or right. . . .

Wherefore it is our will, and we firmly enjoin, that the English Church be free, and that the men in our kingdom have and hold all the aforesaid [already mentioned] liberties, rights, and concessions, well and peaceably, freely and quietly, full and wholly, for themselves and their heirs, of us and our heirs, in all respects and in all places for ever, as is aforesaid.

THE ENGLISH BILL OF RIGHTS

Presented by Parliament and agreed to by King William III and Queen Mary in 1689, the English Bill of Rights guaranteed the English people many civil liberties. Among the document's most important provisions were those forbidding the king from keeping a standing army or imposing taxes without the permission of Parliament. Some of the Bill's provisions were:

1. That the pretended power of suspending of laws or the execution of laws by regal authority without consent of Parliament is illegal.

2. That the pretended power of dispensing with laws . . . as it hath been assumed . . . of late, is illegal. . . .

4. That levying money for or to the use of the Crown . . . without grant of Parliament . . . is illegal.

5. That it is the right of the subject to petition [seek justice from] the king. . . .

6. That the raising or keeping of a standing army within the kingdom in time of peace, unless it be with consent of Parliament, is against the law. . . .

8. That elections of members of Parliament ought to be free.

9. That the freedom of speech, and debates or proceedings of Parliament, ought not to be impeached or questioned in any court or place out of Parliament.

10. That excessive bail [for those accused of crimes] ought not be required, nor excessive fines imposed; nor cruel and unusual punishment inflicted. . . .

12. That all grants and promises of fines and forfeitures [seizure of properties] of particular persons before conviction are illegal and void.

13. And that for redress of all grievances, and for the amending, strengthening, and preserving of the laws, Parliaments ought to be held frequently.

THE UNITED STATES DECLARATION OF INDEPENDENCE

Written by Thomas Jefferson and amended and accepted by the Continental Congress in 1776, the Declaration stated the basic reasons for the American colonies breaking away from Britain. The document also declared the general principles of life, liberty, and equality, in which the American founding fathers believed. The Declaration stated in part:

When in the Course of human events, it becomes necessary for one people to dissolve the political bands which have connected them with another, and to assume among the powers of the earth, the separate and equal station to which the Laws of Nature and of Nature's God entitle them, a decent respect to the opinions of mankind requires that they should declare the causes which impel them to the separation.

We hold these truths to be self-evident, that all men are created equal, that they are endowed by their Creator with certain unalienable Rights, that among these are Life, Liberty and the pursuit of Happiness. That to secure these rights, Governments are instituted among Men, deriving their just powers from the consent of the governed. That whenever any Form of Government becomes destructive of these ends, it is the Right of the People to alter or to abolish it, and to institute new Government, laying its foundation on such principles and organizing its powers in such form, as to them shall seem most likely to effect their safety and Happiness. . . . The History of the present King of Great Britain is a history of unremitting injuries and usurpations [illegal seizures], all having in direct object the establishment of an absolute tyranny over these states [the thirteen American colonies]. To prove this let facts be submitted to a candid world.

He [the king] has refused his assent to laws the most wholesome and necessary for the public good. . . .

He has called together legislative bodies at places unusual, uncomfortable, and distant from the depository of the public records, for the sole purpose of fatiguing them into compliance with his measures.

He has dissolved [colonial] representative houses repeatedly and continually for opposing with manly firmness his invasions on the right of the people. . . .

He has made judges dependent on his will alone, for the tenure of their offices and the amount and payment of their salaries . . . .

He has kept among us, in times of peace, standing armies without the consent of our legislatures. . . .

He has combined with others to subject us to a jurisdiction [authority] foreign to our constitutions and unacknowledged by our laws . . . for quartering large bodies of armed troops among us . . . for cutting off our trade with all parts of the world; for imposing taxes on us without our consent; for depriving us in many cases of the benefits of trial by jury. . . .

He has plundered our seas, ravaged our coasts, burnt our towns, and destroyed the lives of our people. . . .

In every stage of these oppressions we have petitioned for redress in the most humble terms; our repeated petitions have been answered only by repeated injuries. A prince whose character is thus marked by every act which may define a tyrant is unfit to be the ruler of a people. . . .

We, therefore, the Representatives of the United States of America, in General Congress assembled, appealing to the Supreme Judge of the world [God] for the rectitude of our intentions, do, in the name, and by authority of the good People of these Colonies, solemnly publish and declare, that these United Colonies are, and of right ought to be, free and independent states; that they are absolved from all allegiance to the British Crown, and that all political connection between them and the state of Great Britain, is and ought to be totally dissolved; and that as free and independent states, they have full power to levy war, conclude peace, contract alliances, establish commerce, and to do all other acts and things which independent states may of right do.

And for the support of the Declaration, with a firm reliance on the protection of divine Providence [God's will], we mutually pledge to each other our lives, our fortunes, and our sacred honor.

THE FRENCH DECLARATION OF THE RIGHTS OF MAN AND THE CITIZEN

Passed by the French National Assembly in Paris in 1789, the French declaration attempted to define the democratic principles the French revolutionaries believed in. These included the basic ideals of liberty, equality, and fraternity, or brotherhood. The Declaration later became a part of the constitution of each of the French republics. Parts of the document read as follows:

> The representatives of the people of France, formed into a National Assembly, considering that ignorance, neglect, or contempt of human rights, are the sole causes of public misfortunes and corruptions of government, have resolved to set forth in a solemn declaration these natural . . . and inalienable rights . . . that the acts of the legislative and executive powers of government . . . may be more respected; and also, that the future claims of the citizens . . . may always tend to the maintenance of the Constitution and the general happiness.
>
> For these reasons the National Assembly doth recognize and declare, in the presence of the Supreme Being, and with the hope of His blessing and favor, the following sacred rights of men and of citizens:
>
> I. Men are born and always continue, free and equal in respect of their rights. Civil distinctions, therefore, can be founded only on public utility.
>
> II. The end [goal] of all political associations is the preservation of the natural . . . rights of man; and these rights are Liberty, Property, Security, and Resistance of Oppression.
>
> III. The nation is essentially the source of all sovereignty; nor can any individual, or any body of men, be entitled to any authority which is not expressly derived from it.
>
> IV. Political Liberty consists in the power of doing whatever does not injure another. . . .
>
> V. The law ought to prohibit only actions hurtful to society. What is not prohibited by the law should not be hindered. . . .
>
> VI. The law is the expression of the will of the community. All citizens have a right to concur, either personally or by their representatives, in its formation. . . .
>
> VII. No man should be accused, arrested, or held in confinement, except in cases determined by the law, and according to the forms which it has prescribed. . . .
>
> IX. Every may being presumed innocent till he has been convicted . . . ought to be provided against by the law.
>
> X. No man ought to be molested on account of his opinions, not even on account of his religious opinions, provided his avowal of them does not disturb the public order established by the law. . . .
>
> XIV. Every citizen has a right, either by himself or his representative, to a free voice in determining the necessity of public con-

tributions [taxes], the appropriations [raising] of them, and their amount. . . .

XV. Every community has a right to demand of all its agents an account of their conduct. . . .

XVII. The right to property being inviolable [safe from violation] and sacred, no one ought to be deprived of it. . . .

THE UNITED STATES BILL OF RIGHTS

This document was largely composed by James Madison. It consists of the first ten amendments to the U.S. Constitution and in many ways resembles the French Declaration of the Rights of Man. The Bill of Rights went into effect on December 15, 1791.

AMENDMENT 1 Congress shall make no law respecting an establishment of religion, or prohibiting the free exercise thereof; or abridging the freedom of speech, or of the press; or the right of the people peaceably to assemble, and to petition the government for a redress of grievances.

AMENDMENT 2 A well-regulated militia being necessary to the security of a free State, the right of the people to keep and bear arms shall not be infringed.

AMENDMENT 3 No soldier shall, in time of peace, be quartered in any house without the consent of the owner; nor in time of war but in a manner to be prescribed by law.

AMENDMENT 4 The right of the people to be secure in their persons, houses, papers and effects, against unreasonable searches and seizures, shall not be violated, and no warrants shall issue but upon probable cause, supported by oath or affirmation, and particularly describing the place to be searched, and the persons or things to be seized.

AMENDMENT 5 No person shall be held to answer for a capital or otherwise infamous crime, unless on a presentment or indictment of a grand jury, except in cases arising in the land or naval forces, or in the militia, when in actual service in time of war or public danger; nor shall any person be subject for the same offense to be twice put in jeopardy of life or limb; nor shall be compelled in any criminal case to be a witness against himself, nor be deprived of life, liberty, or property, without due process of law; nor shall private property be taken for public use, without just compensation.

AMENDMENT 6 In all criminal prosecutions the accused shall enjoy the right to a speedy and public trial, by an impartial jury of the State and district wherein the crime shall have been committed, which district shall have been previously ascertained by law, and to be informed of the nature and cause of the accusation; to be confronted with the witnesses against him; to have compulsory process for obtaining witnesses in his favor, and to have the assistance of counsel for his defense.

AMENDMENT 7 In suits of common law, where the value in controversy shall exceed twenty dollars, the right of trial by jury shall be preserved, and no fact tried by a jury shall be otherwise reexamined in any court of the United States than according to the rules of the common law.

AMENDMENT 8 Excessive bail shall not be required, nor excessive fines imposed, nor cruel and unusual punishments inflicted.

AMENDMENT 9 The enumeration in the Constitution of certain rights shall not be construed to deny or disparage others retained by the people.

AMENDMENT 10 The powers not delegated to the United States by the Constitution, nor prohibited by it to the States, are reserved to the States respectively, or to the people.

THE EMANCIPATION PROCLAMATION

Although the early leaders of the United States provided for many democratic rights in the Constitution and Bill of Rights, they did not expect or mean for slaves to have these rights. For the first eighty-seven years of the country's existence, slaves remained the property of their owners and had no rights. This changed when Abraham Lincoln issued the Emancipation Proclamation on January 1, 1863. The Proclamation ended slavery and extended the fruits of democracy to those formerly in bondage. The Proclamation read in part:

Now, therefore, I, Abraham Lincoln, President of the United States, by virtue of the power in me vested as commander-in-chief of the army and navy of the United States, in time of actual armed rebellion against the authority and government of the United States, and as a fit and necessary war measure for suppressing said rebellion, do . . . order and declare that all persons held as slaves within said designated States and parts of States are, and henceforward shall be, free; and that the Executive

Government of the United States, including the military and naval authorities thereof, will recognize and maintain the freedom of said persons.

And I hereby enjoin upon the people so declared to be free to abstain from all violence, unless in necessary self-defense; and I recommend to them that, in all cases when allowed, they labor faithfully for reasonable wages.

And I further declare and make known that such persons of suitable condition will be received into the armed service of the United States to garrison forts, positions, stations, and other places, and to man vessels of all sorts in said service. And upon this act, sincerely believed to be an act of justice, warranted by the Constitution upon military necessity, I invoke the considerate judgment of mankind and the gracious favor of Almighty God.

THE UNITED NATIONS UNIVERSAL DECLARATION OF HUMAN RIGHTS

On December 6, 1948, the recently established United Nations adopted its Declaration of Human Rights. Although the organization lacks the authority to enforce these rights in individual countries, it continues to work in nonviolent ways to persuade member nations to treat their citizens with dignity, respect, and fairness. Borrowing from the democratic documents of England, France, and the United States, the U.N. Declaration contains many democratic provisions. Thus, at least in principle, the Declaration endorses the idea of democracy in some form. Among these provisions are:

ARTICLE 1 All human beings are born free and equal in dignity and rights. They are endowed with reason and conscience and should act towards one another in a spirit of brotherhood.

ARTICLE 2 Everyone is entitled to all the rights and freedoms set forth in this Declaration, without distinction of any kind, such as race, color, sex, language, religion, political or other opinion, national or social origin, property, birth, or other status. . . .

ARTICLE 3 Everyone has the right to life, liberty, and security of person.

ARTICLE 4 No one shall be held in slavery or servitude; slavery and the slave trade shall be prohibited in all their forms. . . .

ARTICLE 6 Everyone has the right to recognition everywhere as a person before the law. . . .

ARTICLE 8 Everyone has the right to an effective remedy by the competent national tribunals [courts] for acts violating the fundamental rights granted him by the Constitution or by law.

ARTICLE 9 No one shall be subjected to arbitrary arrest, detention, or exile. . . .

ARTICLE 11 Everyone charged with a penal offense has the right to be presumed innocent until proved guilty according to law in a public trial at which he has had all the guarantees necessary for his defense. . . .

ARTICLE 13 1. Everyone has the right to freedom of movement and residence within the borders of each State. 2. Everyone has the right to leave any country, including his own, and to return to his country. . . .

ARTICLE 17 1. Everyone has the right to own property alone as well as in association with others. 2. No one shall be arbitrarily deprived of his property.

ARTICLE 18 Everyone has the right to freedom of thought, conscience, and religion. . . .

ARTICLE 19 Everyone has the right to freedom of opinion and expression. . . .

ARTICLE 20 1. Everyone has the right to freedom of peaceful assembly and association. 2. No one may be compelled to belong to an associaton.

ARTICLE 21 Everyone has the right to take part in the Government of his country, directly or through freely chosen representatives. . . .

ARTICLE 26 1. Everyone has the right to education. . . . 2. Education shall be directed to the full development of the human personality and to the strengthening of respect for human rights and fundamental freedoms; it shall promote understanding, tolerance, and friendship among all nations, racial or religious groups, and shall further the activities of the United Nations for the maintenance of peace. . . .

ARTICLE 27 Everyone has the right to freely participate in the cultural life of the community, to enjoy the arts, and to share in scientific advancement and its benefits. . . .

ARTICLE 30 Nothing in the Declaration may be interpreted as implying for any State, group, or person any right to engage in any activity or to perform any act aimed at the destruction of any of the rights and freedoms set for herein.

Glossary

archon: In ancient Athens, a chief government administrator.

aristocrat: A person belonging to a social class based on inherited wealth and status; a noble.

civil liberties: Basic human rights, such as freedom of speech, press, and religion.

democracy: A government which guarantees equal opportunities for all members of society through free election of leaders and fair written laws.

dictatorship: A government ruled by a single person with complete authority and unlimited powers.

doctrine of natural law: The idea that certain laws are derived from nature and that these laws apply to everyone in society, rulers and subjects alike.

executive: The chief administrator of a government, often the president.

feudal society: In medieval times, a society in which powerful lords gave the common people protection and the right to farm land in exchange for part of the harvest and military service.

franchise: The right to vote.

fraternity: Brotherhood.

Great Councils, or estates: In medieval times, meetings in which nobles and other representatives from various parts of a realm consulted with the king.

judiciary: The courts.

legislator: A lawmaker.

legislature: A body of lawmakers in a government.

monarchy: A government or country ruled by a king or queen.

MP: A member of a parliament.

oligarchy: A government in which power resides more or less equally in the hands of a few individuals.

ostracism: The ancient Athenian practice of casting negative votes for an unpopular government official, the result being the banishment of that official.

parliament: A legislative assembly, usually representative in nature.

popular government: A government of and by the people.

prime minister: The leader of a parliamentary government.

republic: A government in which supreme power resides in a body of citizens entitled to vote and is exercised by elected officers and representatives.

Suggestions for Further Reading

Neil Grant, *United Kingdom.* Morristown, NJ: Silver Burdett Press, 1988.

Mary Lou Kendrigan, *Political Equality in a Democratic Society: Women in the United States.* Glenview, IL: Greenwood Press, 1984.

T. Mathews, "Decade of Democracy," *Newsweek*, December 30, 1991.

Margaret Mulvihill, *The French Revolution.* New York: Franklin Watts, 1989.

Don Nardo, *Ancient Greece.* San Diego: Lucent Books, 1993.

Don Nardo, *Thomas Jefferson.* San Diego: Lucent Books, 1993.

Diane Ravitch and Abigail Thernstrom, eds., *The Democracy Reader.* New York: HarperCollins Publishers, 1992.

Carla A. Robbins, "From Russia to South Africa, Democracy Fights an Uphill Battle," *U.S. News & World Report,* December 28, 1992.

Mary M. Slappery, *Democracy in Crisis.* Washington, DC: Interspace Books, 1992.

Alexis de Tocqueville, *Democracy in America.* New York: Random House, 1990.

Works Consulted

Anthony Arblaster, *Democracy*. Minneapolis: University of Minnesota Press, 1987.

Anthony H. Birch, *The British System of Government*. London: George Allen and Unwin, 1983.

James W. Ceasar, *Liberal Democracy and Political Science*. Baltimore: Johns Hopkins University Press, 1990.

Larry Diamond, "A World of Opportunity: Promoting Democracy," *Current*, October 1992.

Carl J. Friedrich, *Constitutional Government and Democracy*. Waltham, MA: Blaisdell Publishing, 1968.

R.K. Gooch, *Parliamentary Government in France: Revolutionary Origins, 1789-1791*. New York: Russell and Russell, 1960.

Strathearn Gordon, *Our Parliament*. London: Cassell and Company, 1964.

Edith Hamilton, *The Greek Way to Western Civilization*. New York: New American Library, 1942.

W.G. Hardy, *The Greek and Roman World*. Cambridge, MA: Schenkman Publishing, 1962.

David Lehmann, *Democracy and Development in Latin America*. Philadelphia: Temple University Press, 1990.

Leslie Lipson, *The Democratic Civilization*. New York: Oxford University Press, 1964.

Roy C. Macridis, *Contemporary Political Ideologies: Movements and Regimes*. Boston: Little, Brown, and Company, 1983.

Frederick George Marcham, *A Constitutional History of*

Modern England, 1485 to the Present. New York: Harper and Row, 1960.

Henry B. Mayo, *An Introduction to Democratic Theory*. New York: Oxford University Press, 1960.

Saul K. Padover, ed., *Sources of Democracy: Voices of Freedom, Hope, and Justice*. New York: McGraw-Hill, 1973.

Dorothy Pickles, *Democracy*. London: B.T. Batsford, 1970.

Plutarch, *Lives of the Noble Grecians and Romans*, quoted in Eduard C. Lindeman, ed., *Life Stories of Men Who Shaped History from Plutarch's Lives*. New York: New American Library, 1950.

Dankwart A. Rustow, "Movements Toward Democracy: A Global Revolution," *Current*, June 1991.

George H. Sabine and Thomas L. Thorson, *A History of Political Theory*. Fort Worth, TX: Holt, Rinehart, and Winston, 1973.

Eli Sagan, *The Honey and the Hemlock: Democracy and Paranoia in Ancient Athens and Modern America*. New York: HarperCollins Publishers, 1991.

David Stockton, *The Classical Athenian Democracy*. New York: Oxford University Press, 1990.

J.L. Talmon, *Romanticism and Revolt: Europe 1815-1848*. New York: Harcourt, Brace and World, 1967.

H.G. Wells, *The Outline of History*. New York: Doubleday, 1961.

John A. Wiseman, *Democracy in Black Africa*. New York: Paragon House Publishers, 1990.

Index

About the Author

Don Nardo is an actor, film director, and composer, as well as an award-winning writer. Several of his musical compositions, including a young person's version of *The War of the Worlds* and the oratorio *Richard III*, have been played by regional orchestras. Mr. Nardo's writing credits include short stories, articles, and more than forty books, including *Lasers, Gravity, Anxiety and Phobias, the Mexican-American War, Recycling, Eating Disorders, Charles Darwin, Thomas Jefferson, Ancient Greece,* and *Cleopatra*. Among his other writings are an episode of ABC's "Spenser: For Hire" and numerous screenplays. Mr. Nardo lives with his wife, Christine, on Cape Cod, Massachusetts.

Picture Credits

Cover photo: Library of Congress
The Bettmann Archive, 18, 30, 34, 42, 43, 65, 66, 69, 71, 88, 91, 100
Culver Pictures, Inc., 23, 92
© Robert W. Ginn/Unicorn Stock Photos, 10
Giraudon/Art Resource, NY, 37, 38
Historical Pictures/Stock Montage, 9, 20, 22 (top), 27, 33, 35, 57, 75, 80, 82, 86, 87
Library of Congress, 8, 29, 32, 46, 50, 51, 52, 55, 56, 58, 60, 62
National Archives, 54
North Wind Picture Archives, 12, 14, 16, 17, 22 (bottom), 25, 41, 44, 45, 48, 53 (both), 64, 68, 72, 73, 74, 76, 77, 78, 79, 81, 85, 89, 90, 94
Reuters/Bettmann, 6, 96, 98, 105 (both), 107
United Nations, 108
UPI/Bettmann, 101, 104